GRAND HAVEN AREA

Our People
Their Stories

Wallace K. Ewing, Ph.D.
Marjorie Bethke Viveen, Ed.S.

Copyright 2012 by Wallace K. Ewing, Ph.D., and Marjorie Bethke Viveen, Ed.S.

ISBN 978-0-615-61488-5

Printed by Great Lakes Publishing, Muskegon, Michigan, USA

First printing, July 2012
Second printing, November 2012
Third printing, March 2016

No part of this book may be used or reproduced in any manner whatsoever without written permission from the authors, except in the case of brief quotations included in critical articles and reviews.

Front cover: Martha Duncan   [Courtesy of WE.]

The authors dedicate this book to the memory of Elizabeth "Betty" Davison Kammeraad Dobbie, 1932-2012. Her quiet and effective leadership led many of us down the path of local history.

Contents

Foreword	7
Introduction	8
Acknowledgements	10
Fur Traders and Early Settlers	11
Lumber Barons, Farmers, Fruit Growers, and Clam Diggers	27
Manufacturing Leaders	35
Entrepreneurs	44
Educators	68
Professionals	79
Servants of the People	90
Guardians of Land and Sea	98
Residents at the Poor Farm	113
Artists, Writers, Entertainers, and More	124
People with Unique Stories	147
Index	159

Foreword

The most tangible links to our past for most people are the places and things that remain from previous generations. Old buildings, antiques, family heirlooms, they all spark memories and conversations for a new audience.

However, the stories of the people who created these tangible links are what give them context in the continuum of time. When objects are offered to the Tri-Cities Historical Museum to be considered for the permanent collection, the decision to accept often comes down to the provenance, that is, the stories that firmly connect that object to the history of this place. A beautiful object with no back story is much less valuable to us than a timeworn piece that forges a connection to a person who helped shape our community's destiny.

In this volume, those connections and stories are vividly brought to life through the writing of Wallace K. Ewing and Marjorie Bethke Viveen. Years spent combing through the historical record have yielded a rich treasure trove of data that has been skillfully woven into a tapestry of connections linking the reader to the past, putting what has gone before in a meaningful context that is relevant to today.

The stories, the connections, the knowledge that is passed down from generation to generation is the real foundation of history. The vignettes contained here tell the story of the past in a way that gives equal attention to young and old, rich and poor, male and female, all of whom contributed in their own way to create the special place we all know and love today.

Those who have lived before us are given new life when the collective knowledge of the past informs the present. I hope you enjoy hearing their voices as much as I did.

Steven Radtke

Director, Tri-Cities Historical Museum

Introduction

Blessed by the confluence of three waters, Lake Michigan, Grand River, and Spring Lake, Northwest Ottawa County has been home to a varied lot of people for more than 200 years and to scattered villages of Native Americans before that. As early as the mid-eighteenth century men like Charles Langlade established fur trading posts along the Grand River. Many of these early voyageurs and fur traders were of French origin, born either in Europe or eastern Canada. They trapped and bartered the beaver pelts that were used in the manufacture of the gentlemen's high hats, then in vogue in Britain and France. Grand River and Lake Michigan provided convenient water highways to expedite trading, and several posts were established in and near the future Grand Haven, at the mouth of Michigan's longest river. About the same time that the beaver hat fell from fashion, the opening of the Erie Canal in 1825 and the subsequent push west opened new opportunities for wealth found in the acres of stately white pine that filled the dunes and inland spaces of West Michigan. When Rev. William M. Ferry arrived at the mouth of the Grand with family and friends on November 2, 1834, he came not to convert Indians to Christianity, but to harvest the trees for lumber. During their second winter the small group of settlers was almost wiped out. Their supply ship was marooned on a Lake Michigan island, leaving them without provisions of any kind. Only Nathan White's determination saved them. He walked in mid-February along the Lake Michigan beach to the Kalamazoo River and continued eastward to Battle Creek, where he bought the needed supplies and triumphantly returned to Grand Haven by sled.

By 1860 ten sawmills hummed in and around Grand Haven, sending millions of board feet of finished lumber to Chicago and other expanding markets. The end of the Civil War and the Great Chicago Fire of 1871 greatly increased the demand for wood. The number of mills doubled. In 1881 those mills cut more than 200 million board feet of lumber. Local factories produced wood-related items, such as brooms, baskets, wagons, and shingles. Ship building flourished during most of the nineteenth century, and leather, tanned with byproducts from the pines, produced material for carriage and car upholstery, shoes, and gloves.

By 1890 the sandy hills were bare and Grand Haven's economy ebbed. Fortunately the establishment of West Michigan as a vacation destination had started as early as 1870 with the discovery of "magical" mineral springs in Fruitport, Spring Lake, and Grand Haven. Great "state-of-the-art" hotels were erected and attracted guests from St. Louis, Chicago, and other major cities. They arrived by boat, train, and interurban to enjoy the mineral waters, the fishing, swimming, and the cool air that lifted inland off the expansive waters of Lake Michigan.

Despite the discovery of northwest Ottawa County as a resort destination, declining employment opportunities led to the formation of a Board of Trade, forerunner to today's Chamber of Commerce. Members of the Board traveled far to boost Grand Haven's envious location as a terminus for two main railroad lines and a lake port that could handle quantities of goods destined for points south and west. The first to arrive in the early 20th century was Story & Clark Piano Company, followed soon by Challenge Machinery, Fountain Specialty, and Keller Tool Company. Quality goods were produced by established companies' such as Eagle Ottawa Leather, American Brass, and Barrett Boat Works.

Michigan's automobile industry had its effect on Grand Haven, too, and the first quarter of the 20th century saw Van automobiles and Panhard trucks coming off local assembly lines.

As the resort hotels faded in importance and the family sedan replaced more traditional means of transportation, city, county, and state parks kept vacationers returning for a day, a week, or a month. With manufacturing and resort life both flourishing, the community again experienced enviable economic growth as it entered the 20th century, a period of transition across the country and in Northwest Ottawa County. A burgeoning population, the conversion of farmland to residential development, technological innovation, and the quickening pace of life all lent to the sense of remarkable change.

The European settlers of the 19th century and those that followed them were key to the evolving economic development of Northwest Ottawa County. They helped ensure the continued quality of life our residents enjoy today. The early pioneers are appropriately described and praised in numerous histories of the Grand Haven area. The subsequent generations of entrepreneurs who helped Grand Haven, Spring Lake, Ferrysburg and the nearby townships become well established as manufacturing centers and vacation destinations also have their place in our history. Most of their names are easily recognized by area residents. Each of them helped define the era in which they lived.

In addition to names familiar to all, such as William Ferry and Rix Robinson, this book offers profiles of lesser known residents of the Grand Haven area. Many of them were everyday people with remarkable stories to tell, stories that have been lost in the mists of time, despite the role they played. One example is Lettie Teeple, who kept a journal of her everyday life, telling us not only how she lived, but also how she survived very difficult times. We remember Frederick Graves, an escaped slave who made his way to Grand Haven after the Civil War to find work, home, and friends. Marjorie Boon, a biology teacher, became Grand Haven's first woman mayor. One chapter is devoted to the Ottawa County Poor Farm and the surprising and touching stories coming from its inmates.

Some of the people featured in this book thrived in periods of growth, many used their wits to survive periods of decline. The panoply of notable individuals includes educators, preachers, artists, artisans, dentists, physicians, attorneys, politicians, small business owners, factory workers, housewives, and "personalities," each of whom lent memorable and important characteristics to the community. Many of them struggled to make a living and, in the process, whether success or failure, define our community today. Some were dreamers, some were doers, some were nefarious, and many were common people caught in uncommon circumstances, but these special people, whatever their status in life, contributed to the fascinating history of Grand Haven and the surrounding area.

Acknowledgements

The making of this book has required the help of several organizations and a variety of individuals and families. Images of many of our subjects were difficult to find, and only the good will and resources of others has helped us locate the ones contained here. Essential to this book are the images provided by the Tri-Cities Historical Museum, Coopersville Historical Museum, Loutit District Library, Spring Lake District Library, Hackley Library, Grand Haven Department of Public Safety, Robinson Township, Archives of Michigan, and the Tri-Cities Chamber of Commerce. Other photographs came from Bruce Baker, Karl and Barbara Rowe, Elizabeth Kammeraad Dobbie, Susan Trudeau and Cornell Beukema, Jane Leonard, the Braak family, Catherine Race, van der Molen family, Fortino family, Noren family, Wanda Anderson, Esther Green, Robert Ver Duin, Carol Hall, Bari Johnson, George Miller family, Kevin Collier, Dean Tisch, Bruce Matthews, Van Kampen family, Chuck Rycenga, Wallace Ewing, and Marjorie Viveen. We send sincere thanks also to Bonnie Bethke Brent, who sketched two of the subjects, and to Stephanie Grimm and Barbara Carlson, who provided other drawings. Special thanks to Jane Ladley at the Tri-Cities Historical Museum and to Julie Meyerle at Michigan Archives for being exceedingly patient with our many requests and for responding to those requests promptly and professionally.

Finally, we express our gratitude to the residents of Northwest Ottawa County for their interest in our community's past and for motivating the authors to create this book.

For ease of reading, we have used abbreviations in some cases to acknowledge sources for the images: TCHM for Tri-Cities Historical Museum; PBMO for *Portrait and Biographical Record of Muskegon and Ottawa Counties*; MV for Marjorie Viveen; and WE for Wallace Ewing.

Chapter One

Fur Traders and Early Settlers

The French and English competed for trading rights in the Ohio River Valley. In 1752 **Charles Langlade** led a raid on the Indian village of Pickawillany to dissuade the Miami's alliance with the British. Langlade's Ottawa Indian warriors, some from the Grand River Valley, captured the Miami chief. Under orders from Langlade, they killed, butchered, boiled, and ate the defiant leader. This event set the stage for the French and Indian War. In 1754 Charles Langlade was again on the Grand River, recruiting members of the Three Fires Confederacy. This time he led them against Generals Braddock and Washington at the fork of the Monongahela and Ohio Rivers, where, despite being outnumbered two to one, Langlade delivered a victory. Such successes led Langlade to be named second in command at Fort Mackinac, then under control of the French, and he was awarded exclusive trading rights in the Grand River Valley.

Charles Langlade

Charlotte Bourassa Langlade

On August 11, 1754 at Ste. Anne's Church on Mackinac Island, Father La Franc performed the marriage of Charles Langlade and **Charlotte Bourassa**. The bride was described as "remarkably beautiful, having a slender figure, regular features, and very black eyes." The newlyweds set off in September, 1755 to establish a fur trading post on the south side of the Grand River, somewhere between Government Pond and Spring Lake channel. Cold spray and high waves chilled and nauseated Charlotte, by then five months pregnant. Heir to a wealthy merchant, the girl who was afforded every luxury of her birthright now found herself in an isolated outpost, among drunken boatmen and Indians who disgusted and terrified her. Charlotte's labor must have seemed long and hard. Catherine Langlade was born in Grand Haven on January 29, 1756. The baby was baptized then and there by Father Le Franc, making it the first Christian ceremony ever performed on the Grand River.

Magdalene Marcotte Laframboise was born at Fort St. Joseph, Michigan, in 1780 to Frenchman Jean Bapiste Marcotte and Timothee, daughter of the powerful Odawa headman "Returning Cloud." The Marcotte family was forcibly removed when in 1781 the Spanish raided the fort. Magdalene's father sought his fortune in Wisconsin. After their split, Timothee returned to her tribal community located on Crockery Creek, where she raised Magdalene in Odawa ways. At age 14, Magdalene wed Joseph La Framboise, who operated twenty posts along the Grand, Kalamazoo, and Muskegon Rivers and became a successful American Fur Company trader. In 1809 Joseph was brutally murdered by an irate Indian demanding whiskey. After Joseph died, the capable Magdalene assumed administrative responsibilities for his lucrative fur trading posts, which included sites at Grand Haven, Crockery Creek, Ada and beyond. Madame La Framboise, as she came to be called, was celebrated for her ability to bridge cultural gaps that separated people by race, religion, and gender. When she retired to Mackinac Island in 1821, Rix Robinson took control of trading operations in the Grand River region. Magdalene went on to actively support the Catholic Church and to train young native women as teachers. She died at age 66 in 1846. Her Mackinac Island home is now the Harbor View Bed and Breakfast, situated next to Ste. Anne's Church, where Magdalene's crypt can be seen. Magdalene La Framboise was one of the first to be inducted into the Michigan Women's Hall of Fame. [Sketch by unknown artist.]

Magdalene Marcotte La Framboise

On Mackinac Island in the summer of 1830, Rix Robinson applied for a license to trade with the Indians "at Grand River and its vicinity." Terms of the agreement required Robinson to list aliens on his crew, 17 non-Americans. These boatmen and a single interpreter were dutifully named along with their role, physical description, and "by birth," e.g., Canadian, Half Breed, and Mulatto. Then Robinson did history a favor: he named his clerks, American men positioned higher on his corporate ladder. At the bottom of the list, scrawled in what seemed like an after-thought, he posted "Louis Cawne . . . Woman . . . Half Breed." Who was this mysterious woman?

"Louis" was the daughter of fur trader Pierre Cawne, a.k.a. Constant. Born at her father's Muskegon Lake post, by all accounts, "**Lisette**" **Constant** was extremely intelligent, wholly capable, socially appealing, and of rare beauty. At twelve she began clerking in her father's Muskegon operation and at his post on the Grand River at Trader's Creek near Allendale. When Pierre Constant died, Lisette inherited the business. She engaged Rix Robinson for supplies, some years up to $20,000 worth. According to William Ferry, Lisette was the most successful fur trader in the Northwest and was often compared to Madame La Framboise. Rich and beautiful, Lisette was the belle of Muskegon. A 1937 *Muskegon Chronicle* retrospective declared, "Clad in buckskins, the shapely figure of Louisa Constant gladdened the eyes of whites and Indians alike as she went about her duties at the trading post." More than a clerk, she owned the company. In 1835 William Lasley built a rival post in Muskegon. Soon a merger of the marital kind was in the making. When William died in 1853, Lisette moved to Oshkosh, Wisconsin, where she died in 1907. [Photograph courtesy of Hackley Library.]

Lisette Constant Lasley

Robert Stuart

In 1819 **Robert Stuart** went to Mackinac Island to manage the American Fur Company. It was through Stuart's urging that Rev. William Ferry in 1833 made a circuit of Lake Michigan, stopping at the mouth of the Grand River along the way. He supplied much of the capital needed for the Grand Haven settlement that followed. Ferry wished to name the community "Stuart" in his honor, but Rix Robinson already had registered the name Grand Haven. In 1834 Stuart was an equal partner with Robinson and Ferry of the Grand Haven Company for the purpose of buying pinelands, erecting mills, and lumbering. In 1835 Robert was Government Indian Agent for the Northwest. In 1846 he donated land to Ottawa County for use as a site for the county court house, offices, and jail. The city block remains public land today. [Photograph courtesy of TCHM.]

Rev. **William Ferry**, Grand Haven's founder, arrived by boat at the mouth of the Grand River on November 2, 1834 with family and friends. While he made no speeches about slavery, he was committed to the Abolitionist Movement that preceded the Civil War, and he brought Blacks to Grand Haven after the war. Among those he provided with shelter and employment were Benjamin Jones and Edmon Smith, both of whom served with the federal army during the war. [Photograph courtesy of TCHM.]

William M. Ferry

Pierre Duvernay

Frenchman and fur trapper, **Pierre Duvernay** in September, 1834 accompanied Rev. William Ferry on a canoe trip from Detroit across lower Michigan to the mouth of the Grand River, the future site of Grand Haven. On November 2, two months later, Pierre returned on the schooner *Supply* with his Indian wife, Rev. Ferry, and others. He and the other passengers became the area's first permanent White settlers. Duvernay was an agent for Rix Robinson, but he also sold Indian blankets, fabric, salt, whitefish, cranberries, and maple syrup products. Three of the Duvernay sons served in the military during the Civil War. Pierre died in 1862. [Photograph courtesy of TCHM.]

Rix Robinson was born in Massachusetts in 1789. At the onset of the War of 1812, Rix abandoned his law studies and ventured west, thereby avoiding being drafted into a conflict his father opposed. He became a sutler, supplying troops from a distance. Having earned respectability as a merchant, Robinson was invited into a limited partnership with the American Fur Company at Mackinac. When Madame Magdalene La Framboise retired from the fur trade in 1821, Robinson was assigned her southwest Michigan territory. He built a trading post, warehouse, and primitive home at the mouth of the Grand River. His success as a trader was based on his ability to bridge the gap between the white and Indian cultures, establishing long term, trusted relationships with both groups. He was fluent in French, English and numerous native dialects and was admired for his intelligence and wilderness survival skills. He helped broker at least two treaties. When the Grand Haven area was surveyed in 1832, Robinson gained title to vast tracts of timber land. He and Robert Stuart laid the groundwork for Reverend William Ferry party's arrival on November 2, 1834. Though it was Ferry who is credited with founding the community, it was Rix Robinson who aptly named Grand Haven. Four of Rix's brothers settled along the Grand River the following year. While Robinson established his permanent trading operation upstream in Ada, facilities here served as a storage area and staging ground for transporting furs to the annual spring rendezvous in Mackinac. He went on to serve in the Michigan State Senate from 1847 to 1849. Rix died in 1875 and is buried in Ada. [Photograph courtesy of Michigan Archives.]

Rix Robinson

It was **Nathan White** who hiked alone from Grand Haven to Battle Creek in mid-February 1836 to bring back food for the new arrivals, after the ship bearing supplies for the winter was wrecked in Lake Michigan. Nathan's route was long and arduous. He followed the frozen Lake Michigan beach from Grand Haven to the mouth of the Kalamazoo River. There he made the Kalamazoo his highway, but not before falling through the ice and drenching himself in the frigid waters. He recovered from the soaking and continued his trek eastward, ending at farm settlements near Battle Creek. There he bought 200 bushels of wheat and other foodstuffs from a farmer, paid him, and continued on his search for supplies. When he returned to pick up the wheat, the farmer gave him only 160 bushels, telling Nathan, "One hundred sixty bushels is enough for any fool who pays for his grain before getting it." With the help of men he hired in Battle Creek, Nathan conveyed the bushels of grain and herded 100 hogs overland to Grandville and then down the frozen Grand River, returning triumphantly to Grand Haven. His heroic trek of 150 miles in the middle of winter saved the fledgling community. [Map courtesy of Barbara Carlson.]

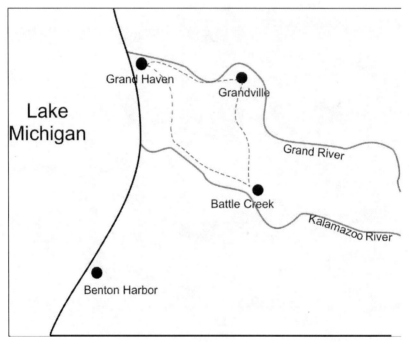

Nathan White's route

The 1836 Treaty of Washington, ceding Indian land north of the Grand River, provided an opportunity for farmers like **Daniel Realy** and his brother-in-law, Captain "Harry" Miller. The pair pre-empted acreage west of today's Eastmanville. In 1838 Realy harvested the first wheat grown here. He paddled twenty-two miles upstream in repeated trips to deliver that crop to market in Grandville. As their families grew and greater numbers of travelers journeyed from Grand Rapids to Grand Haven, the need for expanded accommodations became obvious. In 1842 Realy and Miller built the Midway House Inn. Following the Civil War, America became increasingly aware of its responsibility to citizens unable to live independently. The agricultural setting of the Realy/Miller property, coupled with the availability of quarters at Midway House, provided an ideal location for a "Poor Farm." Ottawa County purchased the property in 1866 for $6000. [Photograph courtesy of MV.]

Dan Realy's gravestone.

Jean Baptiste Parrisien

Jean Baptiste Parrisien, a Chippewa Indian and Voyageur, arrived in Grand Haven in 1835 and the next year became the first mail carrier between Grand Rapids and Grand Haven. Parissien's route meant following Indian trails that started at the corner of Washington and Second Streets, continued in a southerly direction to Rosy Mound, and thence angled southeasterly through the townships of Grand Haven, Robinson, Allendale, and Georgetown to Jenison. His path became known as the Grandville Road. Between 1836 and 1841 Parrisien carried the mail twice a week along that route on foot between Grandville and Grand Haven. Some of the roads he blazed no longer exist. He later carried mail for the Grand Haven Company. Parrisien died in 1912 at the age of 100. [Photograph courtesy of TCHM.]

A survey of the Michigan wilderness was begun in 1787. Given easy credit and wild speculation, land mongers soon made claim. Locally, the biggest grabs went to Rix Robinson and William Ferry. Lesser known were Henry Morgan and **John Allen**, whose holdings included huge tracts of riverfront property and five lots in the "lower diggings" along the city's waterfront. Though the Financial Panic of 1837 crushed their dreams of boundless wealth, the two retained significant Grand Haven acreage into the 1840s. The land eventually was sold to lumbermen. Morgan thrived. Allen eventually founded Ann Arbor and, ever the speculator, was lured to the California Gold Rush. He died near San Francisco in 1851. [Photograph courtesy Michigan Archives.]

John Allen

Trained in medicine in Boston, **Timothy Eastman** was Ottawa County's first physician. After living several years in Grand Haven, Eastman in 1842 moved a few miles east to the town of Scranton. On November 4, 1855, he and his sons platted the town and renamed it Eastmanville. The next year Eastman became a charter member and Secretary of the Ottawa County Agricultural Society. In addition to the considerable acreage he bought throughout Ottawa County, Dr. Eastman owned a sawmill at Eastmanville. He died in 1868 in Chicago. [Photograph courtesy of TCHM.]

Timothy Eastman

Henry Pennoyer

Born in Connecticut in 1809, **Henry Pennoyer** and his wife moved to Grand Haven, where in 1843 he became owner of the Ottawa House Hotel. By the early 1850s he was operating the Washington House Hotel, also in downtown Grand Haven. Pennoyer served as postmaster, Ottawa County's first sheriff, treasurer for Grand Haven, and representative to the Michigan House and Senate. A year after his wife Harriet died in 1852, Pennoyer married Lettie Teeple Rellingston. Henry and Lettie eventually bought a 600-acre farm in Crockery Township, where he remained the rest of his life. Because of his size 14 shoes, the Indians and voyageurs nicknamed him "Big Foot." Pennoyer died in 1886. [Photograph courtesy of Rhea May Hubbel.]

Chid Duvernay

William "Chid" Duvernay, the son of Pierre and Mindoemoeyah Duvernay, was born in Grand Haven in 1851. Claiming to be 13 years old, Chid enlisted in Company B of the 1st Michigan Sharpshooters on December 4, 1862. He was "Detailed as Musician" and eventually became a drummer boy, although he was known to pick up a rifle when needed. When the all-Indian Company K was formed, Chid and his half-brother John Kedgnal asked to be transferred, but his company commander vetoed the request.

A comrade said of Chid, "He was not like the rest of the drummers. In an engagement he was in the heat of many a hard fought skirmish, urging the men by the lively beating of his drum." Toward the end of July 1864, Chid's commanding officer assigned him to duty as a hospital attendant. Known as "Grand Haven's Drummer Boy," Chid was mustered out on July 28, 1865. In 1869, Chid injured his left hand while working on a water well. The 1870 census showed him living in Grand Haven with his mother and other family members, all listed as Indian. He was unemployed at that time. In 1882 he was admitted to Northwestern National Home for Disabled Volunteer Soldiers in Wisconsin. He died there in 1893 and at Chid's request his body was returned to Michigan to be buried at Lake Forest Cemetery. [Photograph courtesy of Thomas Duvernay.]

Lettie Teeple

"Hope is a great friend to the afflicted. Dispair and Hope faught a battle in my brain and hope came out ahead, but not until a great change had come over me." **Aletta "Lettie" Teeple**, wrote these words as part of a journal detailing her struggles to raise a family in early Ottawa County. She was born in 1829 in Plymouth, Michigan. Lettie left home at the age of 20 to live with her sister and brother-in-law in Ferrysburg. On Christmas Day, 1849 she married William Rellingston. By July 12 the next year the groom had abandoned his pregnant wife. Henry Pennoyer hired her to look after his children and to work at his hotel in downtown Grand Haven. Not long after Henry's wife died, he and Lettie were married. She raised her daughter, Sarah Jane Rellingston, became step-mother to Henry's four children from his first marriage, and had five more with Henry. After Henry's death in 1886 Lettie moved to the Northwest. [Photo courtesy of Rhea Mae Hubbel.]

Franklin Everett

For six months in 1852 **Franklin Everett** and his wife had charge of the new school on First Street in Grand Haven, built and opened in 1851 and supervised the first year by Mary A. White. Franklin was the author of *Memorials of the Grand River Valley*, an early and detailed history of life on Michigan's longest river. Franklin died, blind and in poor health, in 1894 in Grand Rapids. [Photograph courtesy of Grand Rapids Historical Society.]

Angie Ball in front of her home

Angie Ball and her husband, John, arrived in Grand Haven in 1851. In the year of their arrival, the Balls and fourteen other couples used two 25-foot canoes bought from the Indians to retrieve logs thrown into the river as waste and with them constructed the First Reformed Church on Third Street, earning it the name "Slab Church."

The church later moved to the northeast corner of Third and Washington Streets, where it stands today. Angie Ball remained a member of the First Reformed Church until her death at the age of 93. John operated a grocery store in Grand Haven. Angie is shown in front of her home at 320 Clinton Street. [Photograph courtesy of Barbara and Karl Rowe.]

Chapter Two

Lumber Barons, Farmers, Fruit Growers, and Clam Diggers

Although his life was cut short by heart disease, the energy, foresight, and entrepreneurship of **Hunter Savidge** led him to heady heights as a lumber baron. Born in Pennsylvania, Savidge attended school in the wintertime and worked in construction during summer. In 1850 he moved to Rockford, Illinois to teach, but soon was back in the contracting and building business. In 1856 he came to Spring Lake to purchase lumber for his business. He liked the area and the next year returned to manufacture lumber. He formed an association with lumbermen by the name of Young and Montague and opened the Young, Savidge & Montague Sawmill. The enterprise was short lived. The financial panic of 1857 forced the enterprise out of business. Undaunted, between 1858 and 1861 Hunter joined Dwight Cutler of Grand Haven and organized another lumbering business. Their firm began to thrive as one of the most extensive and best known lumber firms in the Midwest.

Hunter Savidge

In 1870 Hunter and his partner bought a controlling interest in the Haire & Tolford Sawmill on Spring Lake. The new enterprise prospered from the beginning, and Hunter became owner of a large amount of valuable real estate. The discovery in 1870 of mineral waters on the site of the old sawmill led to the construction of Spring Lake House, one of the most popular summer resorts in West Michigan. By 1874 Hunter's lumbering business had half a million dollars in capital and was processing 50,000,000 board feet per year. Cutler & Savidge became one of the largest lumbering businesses in the area.

In 1873 Hunter constructed the Odd Fellows Building at 136 Washington in Grand Haven. He was a long-time member of the organization. He organized a fire department in Spring Lake, primarily to protect his sawmill. He was elected Supervisor of Spring Lake in 1876, was President of Greenville Lumber Company, became President of Ottawa County Booming Company, and served twenty years on the Spring Lake School Board. He gave this advice to a man who found himself in a financial emergency: "Cut down your expenses and keep cool." Hunter died at 53 in 1881, about nine years before the end of the lumbering industry in the Grand Haven area. [Photograph courtesy of Loutit Library.]

Charles E. Wyman

Born in New York in 1826, **Charles E. Wyman** moved to Ohio when he was 20 and remained there for six years before coming to Michigan. By 1864 he had built a sawmill in Blendon Township that necessitated a six-mile railroad line to the Grand River. He sold the mill the next year and ventured into the oil business in Oil Creek, Pennsylvania. Upon his return to Grand Haven just a year later, Charles formed a partnership with Henry W. Buswell of Grand Haven. They bought the Ferry Sawmill at the foot of Columbus Street, and when that mill burned down in 1868 they erected a new mill a little farther up the Grand River,,and they opened a mill on the Muskegon River at White Cloud. That mill employed about 35 men and produced approximately 50,000 board feet a day. In 1887 Charles was named Director of the newly formed Dake Engine Company, located in Grand Haven. He was one of the major shareholders of the company. Although Charles and his family resided at 308 Franklin Street in Grand Haven, he died at a home near Nunica in 1899. [Image courtesy of PBMO.]

Townsend Gidley

With letters of introduction to General Lewis Cass, **Townsend Gidley** relocated from Poughkeepsie, New York to Jackson, Michigan in 1834. The following year, thirty-year-old Gidley became the youngest member of the Constitutional Convention, convened for the purpose of organizing the proposed State of Michigan. He went on to serve three sessions in the Michigan House and was a State Senator for five terms. During this period, Gidley was also a known agent in the Underground Railroad at Parra, Michigan. His 27-year political career and assistance to slaves escaping north reflected the man's popularity, tenacity, and social consciousness. In 1868, following his wife's death, 62-year-old Townsend purchased 2,000 acres of the Robert Stuart estate located in Grand Haven Township. Stuart had financed the founding of Grand Haven in 1834. At a time when agriculture and tourism were overtaking the lumber industry, Gidley planted 20,000 fruit trees in the area still known today as Peach Plains. To delight and excite increasing numbers of visitors, Gidley and his lumber baron partners built a "Driving Park." The facility included barns, a grandstand, the Club House, and a mile oval for harness racing. Nationally ranked horses competed for bragging rights and large cash prizes. A frightful winter in the late 1870s killed fruit tree region-wide and nearly ruined Gidley. He died in 1889. [Photograph courtesy of BPMO.]

George and Eddie Aiken

In 1866 the whaler *Sappho* took **George Aiken** deep into the South Pacific. Returning to New Hampshire in 1870 and with wanderlust anew, he headed west. Aiken sailed the Great Lakes aboard the bark *Chicago Board of Trade* serving as cook. In 1874 the *CBT* sank in Lake Erie. Following that harrowing experience George sought *terra firma* in his favorite port, Grand Haven. He purchased land from Townsend Gidley and committed "Everlows Farm" to growing produce. His famous squash recipe appeared in the newspaper: "Cut in slices and peal; leave the seeds in; roll in flour and fry brown in part butter and lard; season to taste. Those who have tried this receipt say it is immense." Aiken's life ended on Thanksgiving Day 1916, when he slashed his wrists. He was 70 years old. His bloody remains were found by Eddie. The photograph shows him in earlier years with his son Eddie. [Image courtesy of PBMO']

Harry Deremo

Born locally in 1880, **Harry Deremo** by 1904 was focused on supporting his wife and newborn daughter Dorothy. He supplemented his farm income by clamming. Harry harvested the live unionids, boiling boatloads. He popped their shells and extricated the rare pearl. The meat was dried and fed to farm animals and the shells sold to button factories. "Butts" punched from the shells were polished to create high quality buttons. Any discovery of pearls delighted clammers, and hunting them became an industry in itself. Potawatomie Bayou, located adjacent to Harry's property, was said to be a pearling Mecca for dozens of prospectors camped there. Harry sold his gems to jewelers, fetching as much as $7 to $10 each. At those prices exploitation soon followed. Today fresh water mussels are one of the most endangered animals in North America. [Photograph courtesy Esther Green.]

While clamming supplemented his income, Harry Deremo's primary focus was on his fruit orchard and dairy herd. The Dust Bowl summers of the 1930s compromised both. When his daughter **Dorothy Deremo** inherited the place in 1947, she consulted with the soil conservation experts at Michigan State University. On their advice, Dorothy planted Christmas trees in her sandy back yard, returning the farm to productivity and bringing holiday joy to hundreds of thousands of families nationwide. In the snapshot below, Dorothy is paddling through a sea of lotus blossoms on Deremo Bayou in the canoe she proudly purchased when just a teenager. [Photograph courtesy of Esther Green.]

Dorothy Deremo

George Hancock

Born in England in 1818, **George Hancock** immigrated to Grand Haven and took up gardening in addition to his jobs in a sawmill and at a wagon-making business. He experimented with celery as early as 1866 and was credited with introducing the cultivation of celery to the state of Michigan. In 1872 he started raising fruits and vegetables commercially. By 1897 George Hancock & Son Wholesale Florists of Grand Haven cultivated 40 acres, owned 14 large greenhouses, and was known for its varieties of carnations, celery, and canned tomatoes. [Photograph courtesy of TCHM.]

Klaas Mulder and family

Klaas Mulder and his family pose neatly for the camera in front of their farm home in Grand Haven, where they raised livestock and crops. Klaas and his wife were natives of The Netherlands, where he was born in 1848 and she around 1862. The Lake Michigan dunes are barely visible in the background. Today the home at 540 Colfax Street is surrounded by other houses. [Photograph courtesy of WE.]

William and Dorothea Schmidt immigrated to the United States from Germany in 1866. By 1876 they owned an 80-acre farm in Grand Haven Township. Here William poses in front of their farm with five of his sons. Dorothea passed away in 1903, and William died in 1923. The farm eventually became the site of Grand Haven High School. [Photograph courtesy of WE.]

William Schmidt and family

Chapter Three
Manufacturing Leaders

In 1887, after **Healey Akeley** and his wife had moved from Grand Haven to Minneapolis, the philanthropist gave $5,000 in cash, his mansion, and land in Grand Haven, then valued at $47,000, to be used as the site for Akeley School for Girls. The converted mansion was named Blanche Hall in memory of Akeley's deceased daughter. Born in 1836, Healey at age 22 moved to Grand Haven, where he helped develop the lumber and shipping industries. He was one of the major stockholders of the Grand Haven Lumber Company, and he was Justice of the Peace and Circuit Court Commissioner for two years. In 1862 he founded the newspaper *Grand Haven Union*. The next year Healey enlisted in the 2nd Michigan Cavalry, serving primarily in Mississippi, and was promoted in short time to First Lieutenant, then Adjutant, and finally to Captain. After the war, Healey bought for $13,000 a considerable amount of land outside the original Grand Haven village limits for building sites, including his own "beautiful residence" on Washington Street that eventually became the campus of Akeley Institute. From 1866 to 1880 he was Customs Collector for the United States Government. In 1871 he erected at 200 Washington Street a large two-story frame building, which became known as the Akeley Block. The structure housed several retail establishments over the years, including Slayton's Dry Goods, Watson's Dry Goods, Addison's, Addison-Baltz, and Steketee's, and now is home to the Tri-Cities Historical Museum. In 1872 he partnered with Charles Boyden and formed the Boyden & Akeley Shingle Mill, once the world's largest. In 1882 he contributed $20,000 to provide the Unitarian Church

Healey Akeley

with its first permanent building, and from 1882 to 1884 he served as Mayor of Grand Haven. [Photograph courtesy of TCHM.]

Hampton Story

Hampton Story started producing pianos in Vermont in 1857 and moved to Chicago in 1867. He sold that business in 1884 to Estey Organ and then teamed up with Melville Clark to manufacture pianos under the name Story & Clark. The company moved to Grand Haven in 1901, where it remained until 1984. When Hampton moved to California around 1896, his sons took over management of the family business. [Photograph courtesy of TCHM.]

Born in 1857 at the foot of the dune across the river from Grand Haven, **Herman Harbeck** in 1898 started working for Challenge Corn Planter Company. By the early 1900s the company changed its name to Challenge Refrigerator Company, with Herman as its president. He served as President of Spring Lake Village in 1886 and was Mayor of Grand Haven in 1904 and 1905. He was a member of the Board of Trade and later Director of the Chamber of Commerce; Director of the Grand Haven State Bank and Spring Lake State Bank; and Director and Secretary of the Grand Rapids Varnish Company. Herman was named Captain of the Yates Light Infantry [Company F], stationed in Grand Haven, and he was a member of the Masons, the Peninsular Club of Grand Rapids, the Voyagers of Detroit, and the Spring Lake Country Club. [Photograph courtesy of TCHM.]

Herman Harbeck

William Hatton

Born in Ireland in 1864, **William Hatton** immigrated to New York City in 1886. About 1910 he moved to Grand Haven to become General Manager of the Eagle Leather Company. Under his leadership, the Grand Haven and Whitehall tanneries merged and were given the name Eagle Ottawa Leather Company. When the auto industry switched to cloth interiors in 1920, Hatton started the manufacture of shoe leather. He remained President of the company until retirement in 1936, when he filled the role of Chairman of the Board of Directors and turned over the company's leadership to his son Julian. After his wife's death in 1919, William underwrote the cost of converting the former Loutit residence at 114 South Fifth Street to the Elizabeth Hatton Memorial Hospital, Grand Haven's first. In 1924 Hatton was one of the organizers of the Community Chest, forerunner of the United Way, honorary President of the Ottawa Boy Scout Council, active in the Republican Party, and vestryman for St. John's Episcopal Church. [Photograph courtesy of TCHM.]

Warren Stansberry and family

Warren Stansberry moved to Grand Haven around 1907 and purchased Kamhout's Saloon, which he renamed The Bank. By 1915 he and two partners were manufacturing crochet needles, knitting needles, and button hooks at a plant in downtown Grand Haven. In 1917 they started Peerless Novelty at a downtown address, but in 1920 they moved the business to 105 Fulton Street, where it remained through the 1980s, when it became known as Stanco. Warren was a member of the Elks, Peninsular Club, Spring Lake Country Club, and Grand Haven Stag Club. In the group photograph, he is in the front row wearing glasses. His son, Warren Stansberry II, continued the family business. [Photograph courtesy of TCHM.]

Claude Hopkins

Michigan native **Claude Hopkins**, unsatisfied with teaching and picking fruit on his uncle's farm in Spring Lake, entered business college in Grand Rapids. After graduation, hed became bookkeeper for Grand Rapids Felt Boot Company and eventually was put in charge of sales and advertising. On the advice of a friend, Hopkins went to Chicago where he worked for Swift & Company. Albert Lasker of Lord & Thomas, an advertising agency, asked Claude to write copy for Van Camp Packing. Subsequently Claude created advertisements for such automobiles as Reo, Cadillac, Overland, Hudson, and Studebaker, and he wrote for Miller and Goodyear Tire Companies. He became President of Lord & Thomas and later Chairman of the Board. Hopkins was closely connected to Pepsodent and Edna Wallace Hopper Cosmetics, later becoming President. He coined such slogans as "It Floats," "Keep That Schoolgirl Complexion," and "Chases Dirt." After retirement he ran an advertisement agency from his home. He wrote an autobiography, *My Life in Advertising* and another one titled *The Sport of Kings*. He was a Director of the Volunteers of America and Hope House in Chicago, a home for prisoners released on parole. His annual salary at Lord & Thomas exceeded $185,000 prior to 1920. He wrote a book, *Scientific Advertising*, which was largely autobiographical. Claude named his summer home on Spring Lake Pineycrest. He lived from 1867 to 1932. [Photograph courtesy of TCHM.]

Ruby Barrett

When the Spring Lake Clinker Boat Company was organized in 1887, William Barrett was named Vice President. "Clinker" referred to the rowboats the company manufactured, in which external planks were attached so that the edge of one overlapped the edge of the next one, like clapboard on a house. Eventually William became owner of the business. His daughter, **Ruby Barrett**, born in 1880, attended the University of Michigan, but failing health forced her home, where she worked with her father in the boating business. After his death and the death of her brother Robert in 1950, Ruby ran the business until she died in 1960. Barrett Boat Works, as it is called today, continues to do business in Spring Lake. [Photo courtesy of TCHM.]

Paul Johnson

Paul Johnson, one of the founders of JSJ Corporation, served as its first Secretary/Treasurer and eventually as Chairman. He was on the Boards of Directors of Carlon Meter, Grand Haven Stamped Products, Pacesetter Bank, Barrett Boat Works, Dunmore Company of Wisconsin, and American Supply and Machinery Manufacturers Association of Cleveland. Johnson served on the boards of Grand Haven Schools, Grand Haven Light and Power, Chamber of Commerce, Loutit Foundation, and Grand Valley State University, where he was twice Chairman. He received an honorary degree from the University in 1994 while chairing the organization's foundation, and the conference room at Eberhard Center in Grand Rapids is named for him. Johnson was President of the Spring Lake Country Club and a member of the Spring Lake and Chicago Yacht Clubs. Johnson helped develop the Boardwalk and Musical Fountain, and apparently he played the bagpipes. [Photograph courtesy of Bari Johnson.]

Robert Van Kampen

Robert Van Kampen graduated from Wheaton College in 1960. He was the founder of Van Kampen Merritt investment banking firm and one of three general partners of VMS Realty from 1980 to 1992. He established the Van Kampen Asset Management Company with offices in Grand Haven and Wheaton, Illinois. Robert held a controlling interest in Fitch Investors Service and in Marseilles Brick Venture in Illinois. He started Grace Church in West Olive.

Van Kampen bought lake front acreage south of Grand Haven, where he built several large homes and the Scriptorium, a building designed to hold his collection of ancient Bibles and manuscripts. Robert funded the annual fireworks display on Dewey Hill during Coast Guard Festival. He died in Chicago in 1999 while awaiting a heart transplant. After his death, the Scriptorium was moved to Florida. [Photograph courtesy of Dean Tisch.]

Chapter Four
Entrepreneurs

George Christman

Hunter Savidge brought **George Christman** to Spring Lake about 1870 to work in his lumberyard. After the Cutler & Savidge lumber business moved to Canada, George acquired its planing mill and in 1895 formed the Christman Lumber Company, which sold building materials. His son and grandsons took ownership and management of the company, which remained open until 1968. In 1876 Christman played Uncle Sam in the patriotic play pictured here. [Photograph courtesy of TCHM.]

Derk Baker and crew

Derk Baker, the man with the beard standing at the far right, started a lumbering business that remains in the family today. A native of The Netherlands, Baker in 1870 was employed at a Grand Haven sawmill. The next year, with his brother Jeltz, Derk opened a sawmill of his own at the foot of Third Street. With one 66-inch circular saw and a "gang" edger, the mill could cut and ship as much as 40,000 board feet a day. After the mill burned down in 1894, Baker started to supply lumber only to local builders. About 1912 Derk and his son John built a lumber yard at 722 Pennoyer Avenue, where the business still is located. When John died in 1920, Derk resumed control of his lumber business and hired Martin Boon as Manager. Boon was an employee of the company for more than 50 years. Today D. Baker & Son Lumber Company sells to contractors and do-it-yourselfers. [Photograph courtesy of Bruce Baker.]

Henry and Gerrit Dornbos

In 1963 a Grand Haven fishery that had been in business since 1889 was closed down by a botulism epidemic. Traced to a truck load of chubs, the fish smoked and shipped by **Henry J. Dornbos** & Bros. remained in an unrefrigerated truck over a weekend. Although not the fault of the fishery, lawsuits claiming wrongful death led to the company's closure. In the

1920 photograph at the top, Henry, wearing a bow tie, is in front of the fish company at 614 Monroe Street, standing next to the wagon. His brother Gerrit is standing next to the other team of horses. At its peak, the company handled approximately a million and a half pounds of fish annually, mostly smoked fish. [First photograph courtesy of TCHM, second photograph courtesy of WE.]

Sena Ver Duin

Captain John Ver Duin, a commercial fisherman, was born in The Netherlands in 1844. His wife, **Sena Ver Duin**, also a native of The Netherlands, died at age 74 in 1924. She is shown in the photograph in front of the family home at 322 Clinton. The home today is remarkably unchanged from the 1915 view. The child undoubtedly is one of the Ver Duin's grandchildren, possibly Claude Ver Duin. [Photograph courtesy of Elizabeth Kammeraad Dobbie.]

Born in Grand Haven in 1908, **Claude Ver Duin** became a commercial fisherman and later opened a fish market and lunch stand called The Fishery. In 1931 he published *The Fisherman*, a trade magazine for Great Lakes commercial fishermen that continued under the Ver Duin name until 1991, when he sold it to the Great Lakes Fisheries Development Foundation. With his wife, Claude began operating a publishing business from his home, and he wrote a weekly newspaper, the *Grand Haven Searchlight*, that was printed by the Pippel Printing Company. Ver Duin also ran a Fire Protection Service from his home at 406 Howard and, in the 1960s, from 623 Washington.

Claude Ver Duin

After WWII Claude lobbied seven years for construction of the St. Lawrence Seaway, was Secretary for the Great Lakes Harbor Association, and was a member of Michigan Municipal Utilities. He also was Deputy Coordinator of Fisheries for the Great Lakes Region during the war. From 1946 to 1981 he teamed up with Glenn Eaton and Chuck Bugielski to help organize and manage the Coast Guard Festival. In 1948 he served on the Grand Haven City Council. He was a member of the First Presbyterian Church; Elks; Eagles; Masons; Salvation Army board; Eastern Star; active in the Boy Scouts, and Mayor of Grand Haven from 1952 to 1956, at the same time he was Director of the Tri-Cities Chamber of Commerce. In 1956 President Eisenhower appointed him one of the original members of the Great Lakes Fishery Commission, a post he held for 32 years. Olaf Gylleck was his father-in-law. Claude died in 1990.
[Photograph courtesy of Bob Ver Duin.]

Elfrieda Schultz was born in Germany in 1902. Orphaned, she came to Michigan in 1914 and married Felix Pytlinske in 1923. Drawn to the beauty of the area, the couple purchased land on Stearns Bayou. They launched a boat rental business with a fleet of one crafted by Felix. First to pay was a bulky YMCA instructor, who quickly sank the tiny vessel. Undeterred, Felix built four larger boats and launched anew on July 4, 1929. A rare Lake Michigan seiche caused ten to drown at the Oval that day, exacerbating the gloom of the Depression. Despite local and national calamities, the couple persevered, developing their property to include a marina, dance hall, store, and gas station. Politically-minded, Elfrieda became the first female Election Board member and helped found the local League of Women Voters. She campaigned for candidates and "held court" at Felix's Place, becoming the so-called "Mayor of Robinson." Elfrieda died in 1975. [Caricature courtesy of Felix Pytlinske, Jr.]

Elfrieda Schultz Pytlinske

Herman Schmedtgen cottage

Herman Schmedtgen was a lovable and loathed character in the history of Grand Haven Township, where he presided over the notorious Schmedtgen's Roadhouse. The hostelry was located at the mouth of the Potawatomie Bayou, directly across the street from Germania Park. Problems arose when Schmedtgen was accused of serving young ladies at the tavern. Townspeople said, "The roadhouse is far more evil than any saloon." While he promised to clean up his act, only the winds of WWI could dampen Schmedtgen's spirits. All things German were scrutinized, including Schmedtgen and Germania Park. The party was over, and Schmedtgen returned to his hometown of Chicago. The photograph shows the Scmedtgen cottage as it appears today, located behind the old roadhouse, which has been totally modernized. [Photograph courtesy of MV.]

Thomas and Elsie Morse

Thomas and Elsie Morse owned a bait shop on South Harbor from the 1930s into the 1950s. They carried minnows and crickets purchased from neighborhood boys and used by the multitudes of fishermen with cane poles who lined the south pier. The Morses also sold ice cream and other refreshments. Prior to coming to Grand Haven the couple resided in Muskegon, where Thomas worked for a construction company. [Photograph courtesy of WE.]

Aloys Bilz with family and friends

In 1866 **Aloys Bilz** came to Spring Lake and started a hardware and furniture business with $500. Within five years he had increased the value of his investment to $20,000. In 1871 a fire destroyed his business, leaving him $10,000 in debt. He was saved by Hunter Savidge, who loaned him the funds to restart. In the 1920 photograph he is the reclining gentleman on the left, enjoying a picnic with family and friends. His wife, Alice, had passed away in 1914. Aloys immigrated to the United States with his parents in 1849 at the age of 8. He and his wife, Mary, settled in Spring Lake 17 years later. The Bilz Plumbing Company continues the family name today. [Photograph courtesy of TCHM.]

Gerrit, Edward, and Clifford Bottje

In 1867, 13-year old **Gerrit Bottje** entered the dry goods trade with his father before opening a hardware store of his own at 205 Washington Street. It became one of the largest hardware stores in Grand Haven. When Gerrit retired in 1918, he sold the business to Claude Beukema. The 1912 postcard shows him in front of his hardware store with sons Edward and Clifford and two unidentified gentlemen. Gerrit is wearing a suit. [Postcard image courtesy of WE.]

William Kieft and family

William Kieft, a Grand Haven building contractor, worked from his home at 1003 Fulton in the early 1900s. He served with Army during the Spanish-American War. By 1920 William was located at 1201 Sheldon Road, where he resided with his family, shown in the photograph on a Sunday outing. The signs on the wagon advertise his construction business. [Photograph courtesy of WE.]

During the Great Depression **Chuck Rycenga** sold firewood for $1.75 a cord. His sons, Louis and Chuck, Jr., helped with a crosscut saw. They increased production by using a Model T Ford engine to power a rotating saw blade. This rig allowed the trio also to mill railroad ties that sold for 65 to 95 cents apiece. Brothers Louis and Chuck, Jr. went on to start a business known today as Rycenga Lumber Company in Grand Haven. Chuck is the one with his right arm resting on a log. [Photograph courtesy of Chuck Rycenga, Sr.]

Chuck Rycenga, Jr.

Jacob Braak, born in The Netherlands in 1882, was a baker's apprentice before immigrating to America in 1899. After a brief stay in Grand Rapids, he bought a bakery in Chicago on June 1, 1901, when he was only 18. He returned to The Netherlands to fulfill his military obligation, but was excused from service. On his way back to Chicago, he visited his friend, John Ver Kuyl, in Grand Haven, who happened to need a baker at that time. Jacob sold his Chicago bakery in February, 1902 and went directly to work for Ver Kuyl. After two unsuccessful starts in Grand Haven, in June, 1903 Jacob started his own business, the Spring Lake Bakery, located at 110 West Savidge in Spring Lake. Jacob worked in the bakery by day and at the Holland Honey Cake Company in the city of Holland at night, until he established his bakery business, which he renamed Braak's Bakery. Jacob originated a secret recipe for his famous "Town Talk" cookies that he preferred to cut by hand. Jacob married Jennie Reenders in 1904. They are shown in the photograph much later in life. Jacob retired in October, 1941 and turned the business over to his sons. [Photograph courtesy of the Braak family.]

Jacob and Jennie Braak

Born in Italy in 1878, **Louis Fortino** married Chiara Quinterri, who was from the same village. A friend who had immigrated to Holland, Michigan and started a fruit business, found work for Louis, allowing him to immigrate to the United States in 1903. Four years later Louis bought a small fruit and cigar shop in Muskegon for $25. By 1911 he had saved enough money to send for his wife and their son. Louis sold his business in Muskegon and bought Charlie Spadafore's fruit and vegetable store at 126 Washington in Grand Haven. Fortino named his shop Grand Haven Fruit Company and sold both retail and wholesale. It was the oldest retail business in Grand Haven owned by the same family until it was sold in late 2014 to Kelly Larsen. Still called Fortino's, the store continues to sell groceries, deli items, candy, peanuts, and beverages. The couple to the left in the photograph is not identified. [Photograph courtesy of Fortino Family.]

Louis and Chiara Fortino

Gerrit Ekkens

Gerrit Ekkens operated a small grocery for about 15 years on Lake Avenue for the summer residents in Highland Park, but his main business was the store at 206 Washington Street, which he operated from 1913 to 1956. He quit school at age 11 to work for his grandfather, Gerrit Van Lopik, who owned a grocery at 135 Washington Street, now the site of Hostetter's News Agency. Part of Gerrit's business was making and curing cheese, which he delivered by foot, and he shipped cheeses to customers throughout the United States. He became known as the "Cheese King." In the photograph, Gerrit is on the far right. He lived from 1878 to 1962. [Photograph courtesy of TCHM.]

Martin Erickson

Martin Erickson, who came to Grand Haven in 1924 as Manager of the A & P Market in downtown Grand Haven, opened Erickson's Super Market at 416 Franklin Street ten years later. The store previously was owned by the Sheffield Brothers. Martin's grand opening ad on July 7 said, "We would like to have a chance to earn your confidence and patronage by a trial order on opening day." Martin was on the Board of Directors for Spartan Stores, and he was a member of the Grand Haven Board of Power and Light. He and his wife, Zeta, resided at 1400 Sheldon Road in Grand

Haven. Erickson retired from the grocery business in 1972, not long after the picture was taken. He passed away at the age of 84. [Photograph courtesy of WE.]

Henry Kooiman

Henry Kooiman's first job was making deliveries for the family feed store in a Panhard truck, built in Grand Haven. After graduating from Grand Haven High School, he took business administration courses. In 1925 Henry and George Swart became partners in a shoe business at 207 Washington. In 1942 Kooiman bought out Swart and called his business Kooiman's Footwear, but remained at the 207 Washington Street address until he retired in 1987. In the cast pictured above Henry is the man holding the cane. He fitted many children with shoes using an X-ray machine to ensure a proper fit. [Photograph courtesy of TCHM.]

John and Libby Reichardt

Born in Illinois in 1884, **John Reichardt** taught for four years before finding work selling stationery, office supplies, and gifts. A newspaper advertisement offering Charles Boyden's Book Store in Grand Haven caught Reichardt's eye. Around 1909 he borrowed $1,200 from his mother and, using $113 of his own money, he bought the business. Five years later he purchased the building. Three years after that John and Carl Daniels established Daniel's Office Supply Store in Muskegon. John sold his interest in that business and opened The Abigail, an exclusive woman's dress shop in Grand Haven. Reichardt also was a partner in the Pippel-Patterson Printery Company. He next purchased the Style Shop, which allowed him to broaden his range of women's fashions. Eleven years later he opened a men's store and then an office supply company. [Photograph courtesy of TCHM.]

Jurrien Ball

Jurrien Ball quit school at age 12 and in 1875 partnered with the Woltman brothers in a grocery and dry goods store at 201 Washington Street. Their first customer was pharmacist Jacob Vanderveen, who bought a gallon of vinegar for 30 cents. Soon Jurrien was sole owner of the dry goods business, and his brother Gerrit ran the grocery store, although in the photograph Jurrien is posing in front of a display of Pillsbury Flour. About the time Jurrien retired in 1940, he claimed he was the town's oldest native son, oldest baptized member of the First Reformed Church, and oldest active merchant in the city. He was born in Grand Haven in 1852 and died in 1941. [Photograph courtesy of TCHM.]

Lambertus and Elizabeth Mulder

Lambertus and Elizabeth Mulder, natives of The Netherlands, immigrated to the United States in 1872. Lambertus, a tailor by trade, was an early entrepreneur in downtown Grand Haven. He owned a shop on Third Street, where he offered dry cleaning in addition to tailoring clothes.

Their daughter, Alice, married Wilford Dake of Grand Haven. Lambertus was an elder at the Second Reformed Church. He died in Grand Haven in 1938, a year after Elizabeth passed away. [Photograph courtesy of David Vandermolen.]

Martin O'Beck, Ed Seligman, and John Van Schelven

In 1903, when he was barely 19 years old, **James Oakes** started a real estate and insurance business with James Scott as his partner. Four years later he and Henry Boer formed the Grand Haven Realty Company. Twenty years after that Oakes bought the Studebaker dealership, which in 1933 he merged with Beers Motors. The combined operation offered Studebaker, Dodge, Plymouth, Packard, and Rockne automobiles. He also owned Auto Fill, a Standard Oil service station on Third Street, with John Van Schelven as the attendant. Oakes retired from the automobile business to devote his full time to real estate and insurance. After he retired in 1954, John Van Schelven managed the real estate office until 1978. James is pictured here with two other young men, Martin O'Beck, on top, and Ed Seligman in the middle. [Photograph courtesy of TCHM.]

Govert Van Zantwick opened Ottawa County's first funeral home in 1926 on Franklin Street. Two years later the company was located at 620 Washington, purchased from the George Sanford estate. The funeral home, known today as Van Zantwick, Bartels, and Kammeraad, continues to do business at 620 Washington, as it has for more than 85 years, and is owned and managed by Dale Van Zantwick, Govert's grandson. The funeral home also has an office on Savidge Street in Spring Lake. [Photograph courtesy of TCHM.]

Govert Van Zantwick

Nat Robbins

Born in 1866 in Benton Harbor, **Nathaniel Robbins** was the eleventh member of the seafaring Robbins family of Cape Cod, Massachusetts to bear the name Nathaniel. Nat sailed with his father and at age six cooked meals for a crew. He came to Grand Haven in 1884 to join Chamberlain & Company, which dealt in cement and coal. The same year he became agent for the Goodrich Steamship line, with an office located at Washington and Harbor Streets, and soon purchased the company. He also sold horse hair for plaster, firebrick, and clay, and handled anthracite, smiting, bituminous, and cannel coal.

Nat was one of the founders of the Ottawa County Red Cross, which began local operations in 1909, and he was elected Mayor of Grand Haven in 1914. In 1925 he became a director of the Goodrich, Graham, and Morton Steamship Line. He owned three hundred feet of wharfage near the foot of Washington Avenue and leased it to the Goodrich Company. All railroads entering the city had tracks leading to those wharfs. He also owned a large warehouse, located on the site of Rix Robinson's fur trading post, which he used for his commercial fishing operation. In 1933, Nat operated the steamer *Grand Rapids* and transported passengers to Chicago and Milwaukee during the Century of Progress that year and the next. During the early 1930s, Nat was instrumental in landing a contract to ship new automobiles to Milwaukee on steamers, after the cars arrived in Grand Haven by truck. Nat's successful effort to resurrect the steamship business resulted in "Robbins Day," held on July 15, 1935, to celebrate the steamer *Missouri's* resumption of cross-lake passenger service to Chicago. [Photograph courtesy of TCHM.]

Agnes Smallman

After Grand Haven's destructive fire of October 1, 1889, the Magnetic Mineral Springs resort was renamed the Norris Hotel, with **Agnes Smallman** as manager. Although the structure was not damaged by the fire, the destruction of the Cutler House across the street made downtown Grand Haven less attractive to resorters. By 1905 a post office had replaced the Norris at this site, where today Fifth Third Bank is located. In the photograph, Agnes is sitting on the right. Her husband, Captain Joshua Smallman, helped as host at the Norris. [Photograph courtesy of TCHM.]

Cornelis Verberkmoes

There was a time when tobacco stores were common in downtown Grand Haven. The one pictured here was owned by **Cornelis Verberkmoes**, who manufactured and sold cigars from his shop at 110 Washington Street. He is standing behind the counter, and his son is in front of the counter. The customer is not identified. [Photograph courtesy of WE.]

Chapter Five
Educators

Mary A. White

Born in Massachusetts in 1813, **Mary Arms White** arrived in Grand Haven in 1835, less than a year after the community was founded. She taught day school, Sunday school, and adult classes. The adult classes included sailors, lumberjacks, and other laborers, who enrolled for short periods of time. It was the sailors who spread news of her teaching abilities throughout the Great Lakes. On Saturday afternoons she offered local girls classes in sewing and handiwork. Mary left Grand Haven in 1851 to teach in Rockford, Illinois. Twelve years later she returned to Grand Haven and resumed her classroom role. A history of the Grand Haven Woman's Club noted she was honored in a special way: "Miss Mary A. White was present again on April 22, 1899 and was saluted by the club with the CHALANQUA SALUTE." To make the salute, everyone stood and waved white hankies. Mary White Elementary School was named in her honor. [Photograph courtesy of TCHM.]

Mattie Rice and church choir

Mattie Rice taught school in Grand Haven and Duluth, Minnesota. The daughter of James and Margaret Rice of Grand Haven, she was born in 1862. The Rices were early arrivals in Grand Haven. One of Mattie's sisters, Mary K. Rice, married Frederick Mansfield of Grand Haven. Mattie and Mary were the first managers of Highland Park Hotel, which opened on July 4, 1890. Said to rival the Grand Hotel on Mackinac Island, the large frame structure in Highland Park burned down in 1967. In 1895 Mattie married Otis Bowman Dickinson in Wisconsin and subsequently moved to Kansas City. She is at the far left in the photograph of the Presbyterian Church Choir. [Photograph courtesy of TCHM.]

Mary Bottje

Born in Grand Haven in 1897, **Mary Bottje** received her Master of Arts degree from the University of Michigan in 1934. She joined the faculty of Western Michigan College [WMU] in 1926 after teaching from 1921 to 1924 at South Haven and a year at Wyandotte. At the university Mary taught freshmen physical education classes for many years before retiring in June, 1956. She was the author of two books, "Games for Elementary and Rural Schools" and "Songs for Children." Upon her retirement, Mary was named Associate Professor Emeritus of Physical Education at Western Michigan. She was a member of Pi Lambda Theta honorary sorority, served on the Assembly Committee at Western, sponsored the Women's League and was sponsor for the Women's Physical Education Association. Mary spent summers at Camp Bryn Afon at Rhinelander, Wisconsin, supervising summer pageants and regattas and editing and writing the camp papers. She lived in the family home at 618 Sheldon with her sister Jeanette, who taught at Grand Haven High School. Mary died in 1985. [Photograph courtesy of TCHM.]

William Harper

Grand Haven resident **William Harper** worked as a book agent, traveling for 40 years between Maine and California. An amateur horticulturist, he tended the gardens at Eagle Ottawa Leather Company and was an annual exhibitor at the Grand Haven Garden Show. When Harper died in 1934, he left behind a poem titled "With Banners." It read, "Though I am beaten nobody shall know, I'll wear defeat so proudly I shall go about my business as I did before. Only when I have safely closed the door against you and the rest shall I be free to bow my head—When there is none to see. Tonight I'll shed my tears, tomorrow when I talk with you I will be gay again. Though I am beaten nobody shall guess for I will walk as though I know success." [Photograph courtesy of TCHM.]

Born in Spring Lake in 1873, **Julia Soule** moved to Grand Haven when the family home burned down shortly after her birth. For the next 64 years she lived at 527 Lafayette Street. After graduating from high school, she attended Hillsdale College and the University of Michigan. She received a lifetime teaching certificate from Central Michigan in 1918. Julia taught in Grand Haven from 1895 to 1904 and in Evanston, Illinois for two years, before returning to be Principal of the Ottawa County Normal School, located in Grand Haven, between 1908 and 1917. She next taught in New York and was in Cleveland until 1921, when she returned to Grand Haven and taught American history at the Junior High School until her retirement in 1938. She continued to teach part-time after retirement. [Photograph courtesy of TCHM.]

Julia Soule

Doris Salisbury Wilsberg grew up in a house located at 214 South Second Street in Grand Haven. Upon graduation from Grand Haven High School in 1912, Doris entered Ottawa County Normal School, where she received one year of teacher training. Shortly thereafter she began her teaching assignment at the newly constructed West Robinson School on 136th Street in Robinson Township. Doris delighted in her "modern" one-room schoolhouse, where she was single-handedly responsible for 48 students, ranging in age from five to sixteen. Her most worn text was the *Peerless Reciter,* a book of readings and recitations written for the classroom. Doris was paid $45 per month, enough to cover the $3 charged weekly by the Primas family for her room and board. On weekends and holidays the Rural Route 1 mail carrier often gave Doris a lift to Grand Haven in his horse drawn wagon, so she could visit friends and family. [Photograph courtesy of TCHM.]

Doris Salisbury Wilsberg

Agnes Koster

Born in 1889, **Agnes Koster** moved with her parents to Grand Haven in 1890. She graduated from Kindergarten Training School in 1910, later received her Bachelor of Science degree from Western State Teachers College [now WMU] and studied at Columbia University, New York University, and the University of Wisconsin. She taught elementary grades at Central School in Grand Haven from 1911 to 1955. Agnes, a Church Elder, taught Sunday school, sang in the choir, was a Circle Leader, and was President of the Ladies Social Society. She served as President of the Grand Haven High School Alumni Association and Grand Haven Woman's Club, where she was a member for 60 years. She joined Tuesday Musicale, Spring Lake Country Club, and many educational groups, and she was a Charter Member and President of the Free Bed Guild. In 1939 she and the kindergarten musicians posed for their picture outside Central School. [Photograph courtesy of TCHM.]

Fleda Nevins

After graduating from Western Michigan University in 1927, **Fleda Nevins** taught general science in Grand Haven for 38 years. In 1953 she was appointed Director of Educational Measurements, and she developed educational tools for student assessments during her final 12 years of teaching. From 1943 to 1945 she was President of the Grand Haven Teachers' Club, and from 1953 to 1954 she chaired the Public Relations Committee of the Michigan Department of Classroom Teachers. After retiring in 1965, Nevins wrote a history of Ottawa County Normal School, which trained teachers between 1906 and 1919. Active in the Red Cross blood bank, Tuesday Musicale, and Grand Haven Woman's Club, Fleda also was a Girl Scout leader from 1927 to 1934 and a member of the Triangle Business and Professional Women's Club from 1934 to 1941. She was an outdoor enthusiast, a passion she shared with her students. [Photograph courtesy of WE.]

Esther Dean Nyland

Born in 1899, **Esther Dean Nyland** graduated from Grand Haven High School and earned bachelor and master degrees from the University of Michigan. She was a long-time English teacher in Grand Haven and a member of Phi Beta Kappa and Gamma Phi Beta. She did post-graduate work at Columbia University. Before returning to Grand Haven in 1947, she taught in Tennessee and in Michigan. Esther Dean organized history clubs in the Grand Haven schools and hosted "Old Timer" meetings each year to commemorate Grand Haven's birthday on November 2. She was one of the founders of the Tri-Cities Area Historical Society. She retired from teaching in 1964. In 1936 Esther Dean wrote a book titled *100 Years*, combining a century of church activities with Grand Haven history. [Photograph courtesy of TCHM.]

Frank Meyer

With a master degree from the University of Michigan, **Frank Meyer** started teaching at Grand Haven High School in 1936. He is shown here with a 1946 junior high school class. Frank gave up teaching to join the staff of the future president of the United States, Gerald R. Ford. From 1955 to 1972 Frank Meyer worked for Representative Ford in Washington, DC. Meyer died two years before Ford was sworn in. [Photograph courtesy of WE.]

Margaret Stark was the first librarian of record in the Grand Haven area. She worked for the Library Association, a subscription library with a membership fee of 50 cents and books rented at 10 cents a week. She was born in 1859 and lived with her parents at 232 Franklin. She died in 1924. [Photograph courtesy of TCHM.]

Margaret Stark

Elizabeth Van Oettingen

Elizabeth "Liese" Von Oettingen was born in Heidelberg, Germany in 1917. A graduate of Vassar College, she settled in Detroit before moving to Grand Haven in 1959 to replace Helen De Young as Director of Grand Haven's Carnegie Library. In 1967 Liese supervised the library's move to a new building on Columbus Street, where it reopened as Loutit Library. Liese, who retired in 1979, is the woman standing to the right. [Photograph courtesy of Loutit District Library.]

Henry Beukema

Henry Beukema, born in Grand Haven in 1915, graduated from Western Michigan University and the University of Michigan, where he earned a master degree. He taught engineering graphics for 35 years at Western Michigan University. Henry also worked with the Army Corps of Engineers, Camfield Co., Ingersol Divison of Borg-Warner, Hapman Conveyor Corp., and Prab, Inc. He co-authored more than a dozen high school and college textbooks in engineering graphics and welding technology. Henry was a consultant to the Department of Defense in the preparation of instructional materials for the Armed Forces Institute. He died in 2005. The photograph shows him as a happy three-year old in front of the family home at 127 Fulton Street watching a patriotic parade, possibly the return of Company F after WWI. [Photograph courtesy of Susan Trudeau.]

Chapter Six
Professionals

Wyllys and Ida Walkley

Four days before marrying 15-year old Ida Skinner in 1864, **Wyllys Walkley** enlisted in the Army and was assigned to the Medical Department. They posed in the photographer's studio for this wedding day picture. After the war, Wyllys returned to Muskegon County and resumed farming, but found he preferred the medical field. Ida died in January, 1873, two years after giving birth to their third daughter, Carlotta. Wyllys sent her to live with foster parents while he attended Medical School at the University of Michigan. In 1879 he opened his practice in Spring Lake and five years later moved it to Grand Haven. In addition to being a family physician, Wyllys was acting Assistant Surgeon and later Surgeon of the Marine Hospital Service. He belonged to the State of Michigan Medical Society, the Grand Army of the Republic, and the International Order of Odd Fellows. In 1882 he was School Inspector, and in the early 1900s he was Coroner for Ottawa County. Wyllys died in 1917. [Photograph courtesy of WE.]

Arend Vanderveen

Born in The Netherlands in 1840, **Arend Vanderveen** studied for the ministry, but was drawn to medicine. In 1861, just after the Civil War broke out, he joined the 8th Michigan Infantry and became known as the "boy surgeon." He was named Assistant Surgeon in 1863 and discharged in 1865. Arend, assigned to guard duty in Washington, D.C. after the war, was a witness to the court martial of David Herold, Mary Surratt, George Atzerodt, and Lewis Payne, a group implicated in the assassination of President Lincoln. Arend was also present at their subsequent hanging in the Capitol Prison Courtyard.

Following his discharge, Arend attended the College of Physicians and Surgeons in New York City. He studied malarial diseases at the University of Alabama, where he obtained his medical degree. He returned to Grand Haven in 1868 to begin his medical practice.

Vanderveen was said to have delivered over 4,200 infants during the 60 years of his professional career, and he was called to nearby cities for consultations. He had a horse named "Ned," which he preferred to ride even after the auto had been perfected. In 1869 he married Kate Howard, who also was a physician. If her husband was out on sick calls, she mounted the stairs to the tower in their home at 508 Washington Street, signaled him with a lantern to let him know there was an emergency. A daughter, Marian, married Henry Dubee, another medical doctor. Marian continued to live in the house after the death of her parents and husband. Arend was Alderman for the First Ward, member of the first City Council in 1867, a member of the Board of Health, and member of the Grand Haven Concert Band. He died in 1930. [Photograph courtesy of Michigan Archives.]

At age 17 **Cyril Brown** in 1862 enlisted in the 4th Michigan Infantry and was assigned to the Army of the Potomac in Virginia. Although mustered in as an infantryman, he was ordered to serve in the field hospital. That experience set his lifelong career. In 1871 he moved to Spring Lake with $2 cash. In 1881 he was named Village Health Officer. Cyril was a member of the Ottawa County Medical Society and organized the Grand Haven and Spring Lake Medical Society. He once said, "I drive a car, practice medicine, cuss a little, smoke anything from a pipe to a cigarette, and have been known to hit a cold bottle." Cyril was one of the first residents of Spring Lake to buy an automobile, a Sears Roebuck model. The residence he built in Spring Lake looks today very much as it did in the 1800s. [Photograph courtesy of TCHM.]

Cyril Brown

Elizabeth Pruim Hofma

After graduating from Spring Lake High School, **Elizabeth Pruim** in 1882 was certified to be an elementary teacher and joined the Spring Lake School system. She had plans beyond teaching, however. In 1891 she graduated from Northwestern University Medical School. After working as assistant to the Chair of Gynecology at Northwestern, she returned to Grand Haven in 1893 and became the area's first female doctor. In 1886, she married Dr. Edward Hofma, who set up practice in Grand Haven. The Hofmas, especially Elizabeth, were active in civic affairs and contributed to such community improvement as development of parks, tree lined streets, pure water, and a sewerage system. She served on the library board from 1913-1933 and urged construction of a new library on Third Street. In 1914 the Carnegie Library opened its doors to the public. In 1917 she served as the first Director of the newly-chartered Ottawa County Chapter of the American Red Cross. In 1934, the Hofmas deeded 40 acres on Ferris Street to Grand Haven Township, a natural area now known as Hofma Park. [Photograph courtesy of TCHM.]

Winfield Scott Hall was born in Batavia, Illinois in 1861. He received his Doctor of Medicine degree a year after graduating from Northwestern University in 1887. He then attended Leipzig University, where he earned a Doctor of Philosophy degree. He taught at Haverford College in Pennsylvania from 1889 to 1893, returned to Leipzig, and then became Professor of Physiology at Northwestern University in Evanston, Illinois, where he remained for the rest of his professional life. Winfield authored numerous books on such subjects as physiology, anatomy, sex education, and marriage. Winfield and his wife resided in Berwyn, Illinois, but in 1900 purchased acreage on the south side of Stearns Bayou in Section 6 of Robinson Township. By 1912 they owned over 132 acres in three separate parcels. On their bayou property they built Wynnewood as a place to spend their summers. The fireplace at Loutit District Library is in memory of Dr. Hall. [Photograph courtesy of Carol Hall.]

Winfield Scott Hall

Mary Spurgeon Kitchel

Mary Spurgeon was born in Noblesville, Indiana on January 18, 1912. She and her parents moved to Springfield, Missouri, and then to Terre Haute, Indiana. Mary graduated from Indiana State Teachers College [Indiana State University]. She and John Kitchel met at Indiana University and were married in 1935 in Terre Haute. After having two of her six children, Mary attended Medical School at Indiana University, where she graduated in 1939. She and her husband, also a physician, opened their medical practice in Grand Haven in 1941 at 320 Washington before moving to a building they erected at 414 Franklin Street. Following WWII Mary specialized in anesthesiology. She was deeply interested in local history and supported the work of the Tri-Cities Historical Museum. In 1969 she authored the book *Spring Lake Community Centennial—1869-1969*. Dr. Mary retired from her practice in 1980, but took on the responsibility of Medical Director at North Ottawa Care Center in 1983, a position she held for 13 years. She served in a similar capacity for Glenwood Christian Nursing Home until 1991, and she also was State Nursing Home Inspector for Ottawa and Muskegon Counties. In 1969 Dr. Mary was named "Tri-Cities Career Woman of the Year" and in 1987 the Rotary Club honored her as a "Paul Harris Fellow." In 1990 she was the first recipient of the Tri-Cities Historical Museum "Historian of the Year" award. Dr. Mary died in Grand Haven on March 10, 2002. [Photograph courtesy of TCHM.]

Elmer Shabart

Elmer Shabart, a general and thoracic surgeon, participated in the infamous "Bataan Death March" at the start of WWII. He remained a prisoner of the Japanese until the war's end. In 1996 he wrote *Memoirs of a Barbed Wire Surgeon* about his experience. In 1950 Shabart published a paper linking cigarette smoking with lung cancer, the first physician to establish the connection. Here Elmer poses with his wife, Louise, at a book signing. [Photograph courtesy of University of Wisconsin Medical Alumni Association.]

Bridge over Stearns Bayou

George Rogers was born in Grand Haven in 1844. He enlisted for service in the Civil War at Grand Rapids on December 22, 1863, was made Private in Company E of the 1st Michigan Engineers, and was mustered out on September 22, 1865. Having honed his engineering skills, in 1870 Rogers was commissioned by Robinson Township to build a bridge spanning the head of Stearns Bayou. "Rogers Bridge" served the general public and the logging industry. In time the ramshackle bridge was only used for pedestrian traffic, especially by children attending Clark School. It was deemed unsafe in 1890. Today only pilings can be seen, the skeletal remains of the lumbering industry and early education in Robinson. [Photograph courtesy of Carol Hall]

Born in Grand Haven in 1889, **Leo Lillie** shared law offices with his father and his brother Hugh. Leo was Grand Haven City Attorney from 1915 to 1922. A life-long resident of Grand Haven, Leo is best remembered for his 1931 book *Historic Grand Haven and Ottawa County,* covering the early history of this area. It remains a valuable research tool for local historians. [Photograph courtesy of TCHM.]

Leo Lillie

Robert and Martha Duncan

Attorney **Robert Duncan** came to Grand Haven in 1851. He was representative to the Michigan Legislature in 1855; presided over the Board of County Supervisors in 1856; was Prosecuting Attorney and Circuit Court Commissioner in 1867; served as Mayor of Grand Haven in 1868 and 1869; and was Grand Haven's first City Attorney. Duncan helped bring the railroad to the south side of the river in 1870. In 1872 in Grand Rapids, he married Martha Huntington. In 1913, after her husband's death, Mrs Duncan, deeded to the City of Grand Haven 50 forested acres, known today as Duncan Park. The gift carried the restriction that the property remain in its natural state for the benefit of the community. For most of their lives they lived on Lake Avenue in a home near the wooded acreage. By 1900 they were residing in the home shown here on First Street. Martha died in 1918, leaving the bulk of her estate to the City of Grand Haven. The Duncans had no children. [Photograph courtesy of Loutit District Library.]

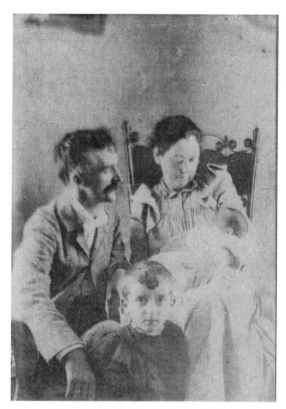

Peter and Emile Danhof and children

In 1915 **Peter Danhof** was appointed Superior Court Judge, but served only days before being defeated by Major Dunham in a special election. In *The Story of Grand Rapids*, author Z. Z. Lydens wrote: "Judge Danhof was loath to part with his honor still so new. When Dunham sought to take the bench, Judge Danhof ruled he could not take the oath of office until he had filed a campaign expense account. The swearing-in ceremony had to be delayed until afternoon." Dunham submitted the requested account, and Peter returned to Grand Haven to continue his law practice. In the photograph Peter and his wife, Emile, are admiring their newest baby, probably Marie, who was born in 1898. [Photograph courtesy of TCHM.]

Chapter Seven
Servants of the People

Dwight Cutler

Dwight Cutler came to Grand Haven in 1847 to work for Gilbert & Company, forwarding and commission merchants. In 1853 Henry Martin of Grand Rapids purchased the Gilbert business and put Cutler in charge. After three years he was able to buy out his employer and go into business for himself. During that time he bought a number of vessels, both sail and steam. In 1870 Dwight went into partnership with Hunter Savidge and together they bought the Hopkins Sawmill on Spring Lake. By 1874 Cutler and Savidge, with half a million dollars capital, organized the lumber company bearing their names and which became the largest in West Michigan. They had lumberyards in Michigan City, Indianapolis, South Bend, and Detroit and employed over 500 men. When Hunter Savidge died in 1881 at the age of 53, Cutler became President of the business. Cutler, his two sons, and the two Savidge sons operated the business until it moved to Canada in 1891. Cutler was Mayor of Grand Haven in 1869-1870 and 1890-1891. [Photograph courtesy of TCHM.]

Charles Pagelsen

Born in Denmark, **Charles Pagelsen** as a young man sailed around the world twice. While on a sailing trip in 1848, he landed in Grand Haven, where he settled and became owner of such ships as the brig *Sebastopol*, partly owned and piloted by local resident Captain Harry Smith. Daniel was admitted to the bar in 1866, and in 1867 he became Grand Haven's first City Recorder, an office he held on and off until 1885. He also was Circuit Court Commissioner for two terms and Justice of the Peace until his death in 1904. In 1871 King Charles XV of Sweden appointed Pagelsen Vice Consul of the State of Michigan for Sweden and Norway and a Knight of Wasa. He helped organize St. John's Lutheran Church in 1866. Pagelsen died in 1904 at the age of 73. [Photograph courtesy of TCHM.]

Eleanor Griffin McNett is memorable for several reasons. Born in Grand Haven in 1850, the daughter of pioneer settlers, Eleanor was a student at the first schoolhouse built on Second Street in Grand Haven and eventually graduated from Elmira College in New York. Eleanor returned to the Midwest to teach in Grand Rapids and Milwaukee and later at a school for Native Americans in Arizona. She had an early love for Grand Haven history and became known as a fluent speaker on the subject. Some of her articles were published in magazines. Eleanor was the first Executive Secretary of the Ottawa County Red Cross, serving in that capacity from 1917 to the mid-1930s. Her childhood home at 315 Franklin Street has been occupied by the Girl Scouts since 1941 and named the Griffin-McNett House. [Photograph courtesy of TCHM.]

Eleanor Griffin McNett

Thomas Ferry

Born on Mackinac Island, the third child of Rev. William and Amanda White Ferry, **Thomas Ferry** was eight years old when he arrived in Grand Haven with his parents in 1834. He learned to speak Ottawa, Chippewa [Ojibwa], and French. At the age of 21 he was elected Clerk of Ottawa County. Three years later he was elected to the state legislature, where he served from 1850 to 1852. In 1852 Ferry was appointed Deputy Collector of Customs for the Port of Grand Haven, and in 1856 he was elected State Senator, serving from 1857 to 1858. Before the Civil War he served on the Republican State Central Committee for eight years and was delegate-at-large and one of the Vice Presidents of the national convention that nominated Abraham Lincoln. In 1864 Ferry was elected to the U.S. House of Representatives of the 39th, 40th, and 41st Congresses. Following President Lincoln's death, he was appointed by the U.S. Senate to a committee that accompanied Lincoln's body to Springfield.

In January, 1871 Ferry was elected by the Michigan Legislature to the U.S. Senate [the established procedure at that time] and was elected President of the Senate *pro tempore* during the Hayes-Tilden electoral count dispute of 1876-77. That conflict was settled on March 2 by a congressionally-appointed committee, which eventually gave the Electoral College vote to Hayes by a majority of one, even though Tilden had the larger number of popular votes. When Vice President Henry Wilson died in November, Senator Ferry became acting Vice President. Because Hayes's inauguration would have fallen on a Sunday in 1877, it was delayed a day, allowing Ferry, as acting Vice President, to carry the weight of the office between Grant's term expiring on Saturday and Hayes's swearing-in on Monday. For that reason, Thomas was called "President for a day" [Sunday, March 4, 1877]. Hayes was sworn in publicly the following day. Another theory claimed that since Ferry was never sworn in, he couldn't have been President, and yet a third view was that Hayes was sworn in secretly right after the favorable vote on Saturday, and that his inauguration on Monday was a mere formality. When in 1883 Ferry was defeated for a third term, Governor Rich appointed him President of the Mackinac Park Commission. It was through Ferry's endeavors that the beauties of the island were preserved. [Photograph courtesy of TCHM.]

Carl Bowen

About 1918 **Carl Bowen**, a graduate from the University of Iowa, was hired as engineer-manager of the Ottawa County Road Commission, less than ten years after its formation. His salary, $5,200 the first year, was increased only $300 during the next 20 years. Bowen first had worked as City Engineer for Holland and then took a position with the State Highway Department in Lansing before moving to Spring Lake. During his 35 year tenure the importance of the automobile grew dramatically, and with that growth came a demand for more and better roads. Carl met the challenge. A bridge over Petty's Bayou in Spring Lake Township, completed in 1947, was named in honor of Carl's decades of service and in 2000 was designated an Historic Place in the National Register. [Photograph courtesy of OCRC.]

West Virginia born and Chicago bred, **William Connelly** moved to Spring Lake in 1910 and wasted no time getting involved in his new community. He coupled his knowledge of electrical engineering and real estate with Chauncey Blakeslee's contracting experience in creating the Long View Resort, situated between Petty's Bayou and Spring Lake [Prospect Point]. The pair's biggest project, however, was their vision and enthusiasm for an all concrete "Grand Highway" connecting Grand Haven with Grand Rapids. The Grand Highway Association was formed under the leadership of Grand Haven Mayor Nat Robbins, William Loutit, and many other local luminaries. Connelly was chosen Secretary of the group and was its prime motivator, earning him the handle "Concrete Connelly." In zealous speeches he told he told crowds, "We want permanent roads . . . dustless, mudless, repairless, and cussless roads." Blakeslee was named contractor. The enormous expense of the 30-mile undertaking drew both criticism and contributions in money and manpower. Month by month, yard by yard the venture progressed eastward. In 1915 Connelly advanced the cause when he gained a hard-won seat on the Ottawa County Road Commission. The non-profit Association agreed to pay the Road Commission $1000 for every mile laid between the two "Grands." Communities along the route were engaged. Though project promoters hit the pavement running, the brakes were soon applied. Fundraising faltered, World War I was on the doorstep, and the Association had extended its inconceivable vision of concrete to Muskegon and Detroit. The "Grand Highway" concept survived only a few years, but building on its logic and humble beginnings it became what we know today as M-104 and U.S. 16, which was completed to Grand Rapids in 1926. Nice, but not so "Grand" Connelly Avenue, which intersects Fruitport Road and dead-ends at Prospect Point, is named for this legendary citizen. He stands in the middle of the photograph, with folded hands. [Photograph courtesy of OCRC.]

William Connelly and friends

Harry Kirk

Born in 1885 in England, **Harry Kirk** was called the "Father of Boy Scouting" in Ottawa County because he organized the first troop in 1914, the year he arrived in Grand Haven. Harry started the first Boy Scout camp in the county, originally known as Camp Shawandosee and later as Camp McCarthy, where future president Gerald R. Ford was once a counselor. The camp was part of a 399 acre farm owned by Patrick McCarthy of Grand Haven Township. In 1944 the name was changed to Camp Kirk in Harry's honor, and today it is a county park. Harry, an Eagle Scout, held the highest adult rank, Silver Beaver. He was active with the Boy Scouts from 1914 to his death. [Photograph courtesy of Bob Verduin.]

Les Brinkert

Les Brinkert's first job at age 16 was as deck hand on the Corps of Engineers' dredge *General Meade*. Les remained with the Corps the remainder of his working life and commanded in sequence *General Meade*, *General Burton*, and *General Peter Connover Haines*. He retired in 1961. Les celebrated his 92nd birthday the day he died in Grand Haven in 1997. [Photograph courtesy of Catherine Race.]

Marge Boon

After serving eight years on the City Council, **Marge Boon** in 1981 was elected the first woman mayor of Grand Haven. She was born in Grand Rapids in 1930, graduated from Hope College, and taught biology in the Grand Haven school system for 15 years. As mayor, she was instrumental in the rejuvenation of the industrial waterfront that had fallen into decay along Harbor Drive. Chinook Pier, the Boardwalk, and Lighthouse Connector Park were built during her three two-year terms. She and City Manager Larry Deetjen worked closely together to obtain state and federal grants to assist in paying for the projects. Marge was named by Counterpart as Woman of the Year in 1982. Grand Haven Rotary awarded her the Paul Harris Fellowship Award. She died in 2006. [Photograph courtesy of TCHM.]

Eunice Keskey Bareham

Born in 1925, **Eunice Keskey** worked at the Pentagon for General Eisenhower during WWII before settling in Spring Lake with her husband, Robert Bareham. She served as Ottawa County Commissioner from 1972 to 1978 and was County Treasurer from 1979 to 1992, the first female to hold that position. She was a delegate to the Republican Convention and a member of the Mackinac Bridge Authority, Spring Lake School Board, Spring Lake Education Foundation, and the state and national County Treasurer's Associations. Eunice died in 2002. [Photograph courtesy of TCHM.]

Chapter Eight
Guardians of Land and Sea

Harley Bement has the rare distinction of serving in both the War of 1812 and the Civil War. At about age 14 Harley enlisted in the U.S. Infantry at "Skenactady," New York for his first military experience. Records show he also served in Dox's and Perry's Company. Bement was honorably discharged as second sergeant in July, 1815. He married Eliza Wood Briggs, and they settled with their family in Ottawa County. Harley farmed, lumbered, and served as Justice of the Peace. Eliza died in a catastrophic fire in 1856. Harley wed Anna Parker the next year. Ever an enthusiastic patriot, Harley enlisted in the Civil War with his son, Harley, Jr. Harley, Sr., was assigned as Private to the 7th Michigan Volunteer Cavalry. Although in his mid-sixties, Harley was in excellent physical health. He was put in charge of horse shipments from Michigan, and there is evidence that he was a surgeon's assistant. While enduring a hard winter in Washington, D.C., Harley was admitted to the hospital with diabetes and chronic diarrhea. In 1863 he was discharged from the army with the notation "should not have been enlisted." After having served less than a year, "his constitution was so shattered by exposures and privations that he was a physical wreck, and upon return home was unable to do a day's work." Receiving only six dollars per month from a military pension, Harley was forced to surrender the farm and in the 1880 census was listed as a pauper living at the Ottawa County Poorhouse. Harley died in 1882. He likely is buried at Allendale Cemetery, where three graves bear the name Harley Bement. [Photograph courtesy of MV.]

Harley Bement

Eugene Gardner and logging crew

In late summer 1883, at the peak of the lumbering era, the financial future of West Michigan hung in the balance. Twenty million feet of timber jammed the Grand River, creating a perilous situation for loggers and rivermen. Rising waters and the runaway current propelled the mass with force enough to shear railway bridges from their foundations in Grand Rapids. Seventy-five million more feet hurled from tributaries into the Grand River, obliterating booms designed and threatening the lives of those who manned them. The last chance for controlling the disaster was on the shoulders of the Ottawa County Boom Company. Should they fail to secure the onrush of logs before their irretrievable dispersion into Lake Michigan, it surely would have meant bankruptcy for the sawmills and their banks, as well as unemployment for lumberjacks, rivermen, sawmill workers, and all the others dependent on the lumbering industry. In the photograph of the Booming Company, **Eugene Gardner** one of the log jam heroes, is standing near the open door, holding a baby.

In Stewart Edward White's novel *The Riverman*, Jack Orde is the fictional river boss at the Ottawa County Boom Company. His character is roughly based on the life and times of Eugene Gardner, who also acted as a technical consultant to White on the book. Gardner, a Civil War veteran, was the real-life river boss at the Boom Company in 1883. His leadership and tenacity contributed to resolution of the crisis. For his guidance and inspiration, White presented Gardner with a signed copy of *The Riverman* and a fine set of dueling pistols.
[Photographs courtesy of Gwen Noren.]

Eugene Gardner in his Civil War uniform

Edward and Moline Jubb

In 1850 **Edward and Moline Jubb** settled in Crockery Creek in an area that came to be known as Jubb's Bayou. Their son Orange worked the farm. In 1863 Orange enlisted in the 7th regiment Michigan Volunteer Cavalry, which was assigned to the famous Michigan Brigade under Brigadier General George Custer. Orange's battalion departed Grand Rapids in May 1863 to defend Washington D.C. Although the Brigade fought in every major campaign from the Battle of Gettysburg to the Confederate surrender at Appomattox Courthouse, Orange was put out of action in 1864. As he wrote many years later, "When the ball struck my leg it was numb and did not pain me for about an hour; after that it pained me fearfully. It does not hurt to be shot, but the after-collapse is the terror. My leg was amputated about midnight, August 25th." Upon his return to civilian life, Orange married Lucinda Bartholomew and started a family. He went on to serve as local Commissioner of Highways and postmaster. Orange died in 1905 and was interred at Ottawa Center Cemetery. Jubb's Bayou today is Ottawa County parkland. [Photograph courtesy of Coopersville Historical Museum.]

The son of Robinson Township founder Ira Robinson and nephew to Rix Robinson, **Ransom Robinson** was a true pioneer. Eighteen-month-old Ransom was a passenger aboard the schooner *St. Joseph* that transported forty-two Robinson family members from New York to Grand Haven in 1836. The boy would grow to be an impressive six feet, two inches tall, towering like his famed uncle. As he witnessed his country coming apart at the seams, Ransom in 1862 enlisted in the 21st Michigan Infantry. The regiment rendezvoused at Ionia and soon joined Major-General William Tecumseh Sherman's division, known as "Sherman's Bummers," at the Battle of Perryville in Kentucky. The greenhorn 21st received "flattering notice from the commanding general for its splendid deportment in this hard fought engagement." After serving six months, Robinson received a Certificate of Disability for Discharge. He had been diagnosed with phthisis pulmonalis. Today it is known as tuberculosis.

Ransom Robinson during the Civil War

Ransom returned to Robinson Township. In 1906, H. B. Jennings said of Robinson, "[After enduring] the hardships of a soldier's life, he came home without a wound. But, hardships of war had left their mark on him, for he was not the rugged fellow on his return, and if he doesn't draw a good pension, it is because he has been neglected by the government." Ransom farmed for forty-five years. In 1908 he was second only to Jean Baptiste Parisien as the oldest living pioneer citizen in the Grand Haven area. Ransom died at his riverfront property in 1920 at age 87. He was buried with honors at Robinson Township Cemetery. [Photograph courtesy of David Robinson.]

Born in 1842 in New York, **Dewitt Ainsworth** at the age of 22 enlisted in the 1st Wisconsin Heavy Artillery during the Civil War. Accompanied by his wife, Frances, he came to Grand Haven from Wisconsin in 1871 to join Wait Manufacturing Company, a planing mill. Six years later the couple moved to Spring Lake, where Dewitt was Foreman in charge of planing operations at Cutler & Savidge Sawmill. In the postcard view above, Dewitt and King Rex appear ready to canter to town from his home on Park Street. Grand River is visible in the background. Dewitt died in 1911. [Photograph courtesy of WE.]

Dewitt Ainsworth

Charles A. Conklin and his classmates

Born in Grand Haven in 1895, **Charles A. Conklin** happened to be in Ohio at the start of WWI. He joined the Ohio National Guard, which became part of the Rainbow Division. His detachment was Machine Gun Company C of the 166th Infantry. Charles died on May 7, 1918 from wounds received while fighting in France. As the first soldier from Grand Haven to fall, American Legion Post 28 was named in his honor. In this 1913 photograph of the Junior Class at Grand Haven Central High School, Charles, wearing a cap, is standing at the far left in the third row up. His fellow students said he had "A hand and a brain to do." Post 28 was chartered on August 10, 1920. It was open to all veterans who served in the armed forces during a time of armed conflict. Charles was buried at Lake Forest Cemetery. [Photograph courtesy of TCHM.]

William Loutit

William Loutit served as Sergeant with the ambulance corps in France during WWI. After the war he worked in the banking business in Chicago, but returned to Grand Haven after his father's death in 1948. He and his wife settled into the family home at 333 Washington Street. William assumed his father's place on the Board of Directors of Keller Tool Company, served on the Grand Haven Planning Commission, and in 1957 established the Loutit Foundation with Paul A. Johnson, E. Vincent Erickson, Harvey Scholten, and John Uhl as trustees. The Foundation's interest was "in providing financial assistance to organizations engaged in charitable health, educational, religious, and community welfare projects" and to "act as a stimulator and impetus to programs." By 1984 the Foundation had distributed grants in the amount of $6.9 million and had distributed the remainder of the principle by 2007. Loutit District Library was named for William's family, as was Loutit Science Hall at Grand Valley State University. [Photograph courtesy of TCHM.]

Robert Bethke exited World War II with a Purple Heart, Bronze Star, and shattered leg. Numerous surgeries kept him from a wheelchair, but not from a lifelong drop foot gait. A chance encounter with U.S. Representative Gerald Ford impacted his life in an unimaginable way. Ford was stumping when the men met. Learning Bob was a veteran, Ford believed he was a good candidate for a government job. Soon after, Bob clocked-in at the post office. His thirty-year postal career was punctuated by the most unlikely event, drawing worldwide attention. On June 18, 1957 Bethke opened a mailbox and saw something doll-like. He stopped cold when a tiny foot moved. Bob extricated a newborn from the mailbox and called the sheriff. The Bethkes considered adopting "Tommy R.F.D.", but respectful of the child's anonymity, did not. In the photo, Bob, leaning on a crutch, shows off his catch with the help of an unidentified friend. [Photograph courtesy of Bonnie Bethke Brentz.]

Robert Bethke and friend

Elmer and Helen Fisher

Towards the end of WWII, Army private Elmer Fisher was wounded in the Philippines and confined to a wheelchair. While recuperating at the Percy Jones Veterans' Hospital in Battle Creek, he met Helen Hidden, who served in the Woman's Army Corps with the medical detachment and assisted in Elmer's rehabilitation. Their ensuing romance culminated in marriage in Grand Haven in 1946. This 1951 news photo shows Helen helping her husband through the woods on a hunting expedition. Elmer passed away in 1976. [Photograph courtesy of WE.]

Wreck of the *Akeley*

David Miller, born in Detroit in 1837, was the son of Captain Henry "Harry" and Elizabeth Realy Miller. As an infant, David moved with his family to Eastmanville and a few years later to Spring Lake. He started sailing with his father in 1850. His younger brother Daniel operated the tow barge *Mary Boice*. In September, 1861 David enlisted in the Fourth California Cavalry. After the war he returned to Grand Haven.

On November 13, 1883, the steam barge *H.C. Akeley* foundered off the shores of Saugatuck, carrying a load of corn from Chicago, as shown in this picture. David was Master of the schooner *Driver* and his brother Daniel was Mate. With the help of Pat Daley, the brothers were able to save all but six of the crew on the *Akeley*. For their heroic actions, David received a silver medal for "distinguished service in saving lives," and Daniel and Pat were given gold medals. The steam barge, built in Grand Haven in 1881, was named for local businessman Healey Akeley. [Photograph courtesy of WE.]

Raymond O'Malley and Coast Guard officer

Born in 1920, **Raymond O'Malley** of Chicago, on the left, was one of two hands to survive the sinking of the Coast Guard Cutter *Escanaba* in June, 1943. Seaman 1st Class at the time, Raymond, , returned to Grand Haven each year to attend a ceremony sponsored by the Coast Guard that commemorated the sinking of the *Escanaba* until he passed away in Chicago in 2007. The *Escanaba* was the first Coast Guard cutter to be stationed in Grand Haven, arriving in a blizzard in December, 1932. When the *Escanaba* was called to duty at the start of WWII she was put in a shipyard, painted with camouflage colors, fitted with guns and depth charges, and had her mast removed. The ship then went on convoy duty in the North Atlantic. After the war the cutter's mast was placed in Escanaba Park and maintained by the Boy Scouts. [Photograph courtesy of TCHM.]

Joe Sickman and firefighter crew

Grand Haven's first full-time firefighter was **Joe Sickman**. Hired in 1919 at a wage of $20 a week, he was assigned the task of operating the city's first motor-driven pumper truck. At that time the fire fighters worked out of a station on the southwest corner of Washington and Fifth Streets. The department had continued to use horses until it was determined that the truck could make the run faster. Joe's schedule was 14 days on and then a day off. His first mechanized run was to a fire at the Railroad Saloon on the corner of Fourth and Jackson Streets, opposite the Pere Marquette Depot. Sickman, nearing the end of his career, is standing in the back center in front of the fire station when it stood at 18 North Fifth Street. Born in Grand Haven in 1890, Joe passed away in 1971. [Photograph courtesy of TCHM.]

Emil Klempel and mates

Emil Klempel was born in 1889 in Grand Haven, the son of immigrant parents. He served with the Grand Haven Police Department from 1917 to 1953. At that time the police station was located in the City Hall on the southwest corner of Washington and Fifth Streets. The Fire Department also was located there. In 1937 both departments moved into a new $67,169 police-fire building at 18 North Fifth Street. He appears in the top middle of this undated photograph. The other police officers are not identified. Emil's nephew, Richard Klempel joined the force in 1947 and was Chief from 1955 to 1984. Emil died in 1965. [Photograph courtesy of TCHM.]

Police Officer **Scott Flahive** was shot and killed by Keith Harbin while making what he thought was a routine traffic stop on Beacon Boulevard the night of December 13, 1994. Harbin and others had made a violent escape from the County Jail in downtown Grand Haven and were making a speedy exit from the city. Harbin was caught and convicted of the murder. A memorial marks the spot where Scott was slain. Scott was born in Grand Haven in 1966. [Photograph courtesy of Grand Haven Department of Public Safety.]

Scott Flahive

Chapter Nine
Residents at the Poor Farm

Harry Miller's headstone

Henry "Harry" Miller was one of the most endearing characters associated with the Poor Farm. Born in Lubeck, Germany in 1811, by eight he was sailing on commercial vessels. In 1833 Miller landed in Detroit, where he married Daniel Realy's sister, Elizabeth. Miller plied the Great Lakes supplying fur traders, including those along the Grand River. Impressed with the area, he partnered with Realy, preempted land, and brought their families to present-day Eastmanville in 1837. Henry Miller, Jr. was born the next year, died at age five, and was the first to be buried at Eastmanville Cemetery. Realy, his wife and five of six children would eventually be interred there as well. In better times Miller recalled that "Indians were frequent visitors to our homes, coming in their native costumes: legging striped gaily, moccasins, skirts, and blankets. They made baskets of all kinds and shapes, many ornamented with porcupine quills in native dyes, some beadwork, and tanned deerskin. Sometimes Chief Motspie was a little better dressed than others, but tall, stately, graceful. They would say 'Indian hungry, wants bread and meat, very cold today, white man.' It did grieve me to see the way red friends degraded themselves by begging, but I wonder just how much they were to blame."

After the farm was sold to Ottawa County in 1866, Miller continued sailing. He captained the *Manhattan, St. Joseph, Porcupine/Caroline, Enterprise,* and *Ottawa* hauling freight and lumber. Passengers were charmed by their able and entertaining skipper. While he tolerated no foolishness as master of ships, in pleasant weather Miller gathered farers on deck to share tales and lead songs by favored composer, Harry Bluff, hence a second nickname, Captain Bluff. Elizabeth died one year before Captain Miller's retirement. In 1861 he married Mary Daniels and the two were appointed keepers of the Grand Haven lighthouse, she being the first female "wickie" in Grand Haven's history.

In 1872 Harry became ill, making Mary central to the light's care. When Captain Miller died in 1876, a local newspaper seemed certain of his fate: "If there ever was one clothed with the garment of hope amounting almost to assurance of safety thereafter, it was Harry Bluff. May we not hope that a similar mantle is waiting those two sons of holy names, as a passport when they slip from the sea of life to greet their Father on the shores of his happy home." Harry was buried with his first wife at Spring Lake Cemetery. His headstone is shown in the photograph. [Photograph courtesy of MV.]

Poor Farm

Pieter Ploeg married Maria Littooij in 1881. The couple raised seventeen children. In 1855 Pieter abandoned his family and emigrated from The Netherlands to America. If he sought fortune, it did not materialize. He died at the Poor Farm from the "effects of hard drinking."

His great-grandson, Reverend Gerrit Sheeres, shared a clipping from the *Holland City News* dated June 1, 1878, which read: "Old Mr. Pieter Ploeg, died at the County Poor Farm, on the 16th inst., at the ripe age of 78 years. He was confined to his bed for the last three months, and one of the directors of the poor informed us that the old man finally got reconciled to his lot, was very submissive and contrite and was continually seen reading and studying the Holy Scriptures, and the director expressed the hope that his end was all that could be wished for." Pieter's final abode, the Poor Farm, is pictured here much as he would have known it. [Photograph courtesy of Archives of Holland.]

Twenty-two year old **Hendrika Vander Sticht** was deposited at the Ottawa County Poor Farm on July 26, 1869 by an unknown person. Uncommunicative and in a world of her own, three months later Hendrika was transported to the Michigan Insane Asylum in Kalamazoo, where she remained for five years before being returned to the Poor Farm. There she resided for the next thirty-two years, outliving numerous keepers, caretakers, and nearly all other inmates. On October 25, 1907, the County Board of Supervisors received its monthly report on the Poor Farm. The case of "Hendrikie" was raised. She was an old woman, "practically an imbecile."

Hendrika Vander Sticht's death certificate

A little shelter and yard had been prepared for Hendrika, where she could enjoy a grassy plot and grow potatoes. She only mumbled. She seldom caused problems and was considered harmless. She played like a contented child. Her case had not advanced and seemed hopeless. Board members, having no knowledge of her complete history, wondered if she might be a candidate for the asylum in Kalamazoo. Would a change in methods help her? "Hendrikie" was spared a second trip to the asylum in a tight vote. In 1908 she died of Bright's Disease at age sixty-one. No one claimed Hendrika's remains. In keeping with the Michigan Anatomy Act, her corpse was shipped to the medical school in Ann Arbor. All that was given Hendrika in life was now repaid in death, with the hope that the next generation of doctors would better understand "Hendrikas" everywhere. [Image courtesy of Loutit Library.]

Poor Farm Memorial Cemetery
In Memory of Isaac Kramer and others buried here.
Dedicated July 10, 2010

Name	Year	Name	Year	Name	Year
ALRICH, MATTAUS	1907	HUBBARD, FLOYD	1916	PRENE, WILLIAM	1917
ANDERSON, JOHN	1884	HUNGERFORD, ASA	1901	RICKNER, REUBEN	1910
AUSSICAR, CHARLES	1896	JACKS, PETER JOHNSTON	1921	RIPPENSPELDER, PETER	1928
BREMAN, WARREN	1923	JOHNSON, CHARLES	1911	ROSIER, HORACE	1931
BOUWKAMP, WILLIAM	1918	JOHNSON, WILLIAM	1916	SCHIFALBEIN, JOHN	1922
BRADLEY, ELIZABETH	1926	KAMP, DICK	1900	SEIBERT, LOUISE	1914
BREARLEY, CHARLES	1921	KORNOELJE, JAN	1909	SMITH, JOHN	1918
BUCK, JOSEPH	1913	KORTZ, JOHN	1910	SMITH, WILLIAM	1909
BUDD, JAMES	1914	KRAMER, ABRAHAM	1917	*SMOOR, GERT	1916
BURTHUISE, HENRY	1904	KRAMER, GEORGE	1919	SONDEY, JACOBUS	1897
CHAPMAN, WILLIAM	1920	KRAMER, ISAAC	1899	SPANG, JOSEPH	1904
COON, LEWIS	1919	KRATZ, MARTIN	1912	SPARKS, EUGENE	1898
CRAPSY, ED	1927	KWAAST, HENRY	1920	TUBBS, RAMSON	1912
CROCKER, GEORGE	1922	LEPP, HENRY	1925	VANDERWERT, WIEBE	1901
DEVRIES, CORNELIUS	1907	LEPP, SUSAN	1920	VANLIERE, DICK	1916
DEVRIES, JACOB	1926	MCFARLAND, WM.	1913	VISSER, JOHN	1899
*DICK, ROBERT C.	1913	MILLER, JAMES	1922	WARREN, GEORGE	1907
EVERT, BERT	1898	MURPHY, PETER	1925	*WASSENAAR, T.	1916
FANNER, BENJAMIN	1899	MUSTERDYKE, WILLIAM	1901	*WOLSTRON, JOHN	1917
HAMMON, JOHN	1900	NAAJI, ISAAC	1912	WOOLENGA, GEORGE W.	1909
HARTIGAN, PATRICK	1896	OXNER, JOSEPH	1916	* INDICATES ORIGINAL BURIAL MARKER IN PLACE.	
HOOK, JAMES	1906	PECK, FANNIE EMELINE	1899		

"Show me your burial grounds and I'll show you a measure of the civility of a community." - Benjamin Franklin

WHILE THERE IS NO DOCUMENTATION TO SUPPORT IT, OTHERS MAY ALSO BE BURIED HERE.

Bronze memorial at the Poor Farm

In the years before **Benjamin Fanner** was logged in the old leather bound ledger at the Ottawa County Poor Farm, he was auctioned at a town meeting to the *lowest* bidder. He received room and board in exchange for light labor. Institutionalization offered Ben a safe and stable place to live. Upon intake to the Poor Farm, Keeper H.S. Taft noted that this homeless and simple-minded man was "foolish and here for life." In fact, by 1898 Ben had been an inmate at the Poor Farm longer than any other resident. He died the following year, and when neither friends nor family claimed his remains, Ben was interred on the farm. Expenses for his burial included $2.00 for embalming fluid, $12.50 for a casket, box, and burial robe, and $1.50 for the services of a minister. Benjamin Fanner is remembered along with 63 other indigents on the brass plaque at the hilltop cemetery.

We rose and rushed unto her aid,
White faces sank into the grave,
Black faces, too, and all were brave,
Their red blood thrilled Columbia's heart;
It could not tell the two apart.

Jonathon Robertson, *Michigan in the War*

Benjamin Jones headstone

Born into slavery in 1824, **Benjamin Jones** journeyed from Tennessee to Grand Haven prior to the Civil War, probably under the guidance of Abolitionist Reverend William Ferry. In 1863 Jones enlisted in the 1st Michigan Colored Infantry, later known as the 102nd U.S. Colored Infantry. He would have been an impressive soldier. Jones was described as a well-informed gentleman having a massive physique and powerful appearance. He fought, was injured repeatedly, and finally was mustered out of service in Charleston, South Carolina in September 1865. Returning to Grand Haven, he worked in the Ferry household through the 1870s. By 1880 Jones owned a farm on Pennoyer Avenue near Beech Tree. Ben was an engaging conversationalist whose stories of slavery and war captured the interest of locals. Over time, lingering war wounds and chronic illness compromised Ben's ability to live independently. In 1912 he was admitted to the Ottawa County Poor Farm. His care was covered by a $20.00 monthly pension earned for service to his country. Old and bent, Benjamin Jones died at the Poor Farm on June 30, 1913. His funeral was held at the Congregational Church in Grand Haven and was well attended by members of the Weatherwax Post of the Grand Army of the Republic. Ben was buried with military honors in the G.A.R. plot at Lake Forest Cemetery. [Photograph courtesy of MV.]

> **No Fabulous Fortune Found**
>
> Dr. Arthur Turner, city health officer and City Marshal John Welch, have been engaged in cleaning up the Harvey Blount residence during the last few days. For some time there have been many complaints as the filth and stench arising from the place. Several attempts have been made to clean up the place, but the overhauling which the place received this time was complete. All of the dirt and accumulation was burned, and the entire place rooted and dug out.

Harvey Blount news article

Harvey Blount, aided by Reverend William Ferry, arrived in Grand Haven in the late 1860s. A 1912 article in the *Grand Haven Daily Tribune* observed that Harvey, who was Black, "went to school at various times in his life even after he had grown to middle age, and he had acquired more knowledge than many gave him credit for." He was one of several local Blacks elected to attend an Equal Rights Conference held in Grand Rapids in 1894. When Blount became old and sick, he was found living amid "filth and stench," officials removed him to the Ottawa County Poor Farm and later to the state insane asylum in Kalamazoo, where he died. His house was ransacked when looters suspected a hidden fortune. They found nothing. [Newspaper excerpt from *Grand Haven Daily Tribune*, August 20, 1912.]

Joe Steel

In late winter 1907 a tatterdemalion was found wandering Lamont, a few miles east of Grand Haven. Half clothed at 5'1"and weighing just 110 pounds, the man was near hyperthermia, did not know where he was or why, and was without identification or funds. He could not remember his name nor any family names. He was taken to the Poor Farm, where all he recalled was having two oxen named "Duke" and "Dime." The Poor Farm keeper dubbed the amnesiac "Joe," guessed his age to be 44, and because he was last seen working at Steel's Landing, gave him the surname "Steel." **Joe Steel** was diagnosed "insane."

He integrated easily into his adoptive family, and the search for his true identity was gradually abandoned. Joe, a friendly man of few words, was an able and willing worker. He particularly liked tinkering with farm machinery. Decades passed.

By 1965 Joe had lived at the farm for 58 years. A journalist visiting the institution that year asked, "Who's your oldest resident?" Joe's strange story unfolded on the front page of the *Holland Sentinel*, and the public was challenged to solve his mystery.

"I am positive Joe Steel is my uncle," one caller claimed. Monroe Eaton had frequently heard his mother lament the disappearance of her brother, Monroe Rutty, in whose memory Eaton had been named. The family Bible posted Rutty's birth date as March 31, 1860. He left for employment in the north woods in 1882. Years rolled by without knowing his fate. Was Joe Steel actually Monroe Rutty?

A meeting of Eaton and Steel was inevitable. The strangers fumbled to find common ground. Eaton reminisced about the family's fine oxen. Did Joe remember "Duke" and "Dime?" Yes! Mining for greater proofs, Eaton asked, "Does 'Little Mony' mean anything to you?" The old man's eyes softened. "They called me 'Little Mony' when I was a boy." There could be little doubt that 104-year-old Joe Steel was Monroe Rutty.

Joe celebrated seven more birthdays surrounded by family and friends at the Poor Farm. His 110th birthday included greetings from Governor Milliken and President Nixon. NBC news anchor, David Brinkley even kept tabs on Joe. When he died in 1971 at age 111, Joe Steel was the oldest man in Michigan. [Sketch courtesy of Bonnie Bethke Brentz.]

Lawrence Smith was estranged from his family in Oceana County and hopped a rail for Coopersville. Standing at Dennison Corners, Smith put a gun to his temple and pulled the trigger. According to the *Coopersville Observer* he presented "a horrible sight." Amazingly, Smith survived. He was lifted to a nearby home, treated, and transported to the Poor Farm. Four days later he died. Smith's remains were shipped to the University of Michigan medical school. Case closed? County officials received a letter months later reading, "Lawrence Smith shot himself on 28th of May 1902, and was carried to my residence by order of the sheriff and doctor attending him." The writer, John Cooper, claimed the "infusion of blood" had destroyed his property. He sought compensation and was awarded $6. [Death Certificate from Ottawa County, Michigan records.]

Lawrence Smith death certificate

> Nearer the end of life,
> Nearer the grave;
> If I were to die tonight;
> I would be brave.

David Fletcher Hunton

One fall day in 1909, **David Fletcher Hunton** brought a sealed packet to the *Grand Haven Tribune* office with instructions that it not be opened until after his death. Six years later, at age 91, David died. The *Tribune* soon discovered that the mysterious packet contained the judge's autobiography. David Fletcher Hunton was born in New Hampshire. He studied law, was admitted to the bar in 1850, and by 1866 had set up a criminal law practice in Grand Haven. He won most cases, but despite a hard fought battle, Attorney Hunton could not spare his incorrigible client, Will Bell. The wayward youth was convicted of stealing his grandmother's eye glasses and was sentenced to the penitentiary. That loss notwithstanding, Hunton was elected police judge in 1902. His reputation as a lawman was equaled only by his fame as a poet. He is credited with over five hundred poems, including the lines quoted here. David outlived four wives. He died at the Poor Farm where, unable to live independently, he had been placed. He dispelled the myth that all Poor Farm residents were poor. Not Hunton. A simple graveside service at Lake Forest Cemetery marked his passing, but his poetry recalled happier times.

> I've had my dreams and they were sweet,
> And all my joys, they've been complete.
> W'en since I've been growing old,
> I've had pleasures manifold.
> So down life's stream I gently glide,
> For God knows I am satisfied.

[Sketch courtesy of Bonnie Bethke Brentz.]

Eddie Aiken

George Aiken was a successful agriculturalist with extensive orchards in Peach Plains, just east of Grand Haven. Amelia, George's wife, bore a son in 1886. **Eddie Aiken** was a frail, compact kid, vulnerable to bullies. Yet the boy showed promise. He experimented with peanut cultivation, grew record-size vegetables, and worked the sandy soil as well as anyone. The downward spiral began with his father's suicide. Eddie was first on the bloody scene. Unable to manage the large farm alone, it was sold in 1921. Eddie worked at odd jobs and, taking advantage of his slight proportions, became a steeplejack of note. He married Myrtle Stone in 1923, but lost her and their small home during the Great Depression. On March 10, 1932 the poor man was admitted to the Infirmary until he could get back on his feet. [Photograph courtesy of TCHM.]

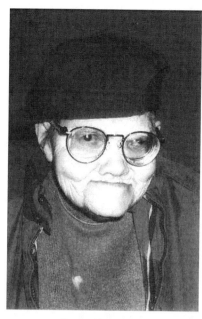

Bruce Regester

[Photograph courtesy of Dr. David Regester.]

Bruce Regester was diagnosed with a developmental disability not long after his birth in 1938. His parents made the heart-wrenching decision to institutionalize him at age ten. Bruce resided at the Pennhurst State Hospital for decades with thousands of others similarly impaired. When family members moved from Pennsylvania to Spring Lake, Bruce was transferred to Community Haven. By then in his forties, Bruce had clever ways of extracting cash from folks and charming them into believing it was in their best interest, earning him the handle "Uncle Bucks." In exchange for a dollar or two he'd play a few riffs on his cherished harmonica. "Uncle Bucks" took pride in working at Community Haven's country store and upon his death in 2002, his cremains were buried at the four corners of that tiny building.

A poem by Dr. David Regester honored his brother Bruce:

View from the Bench

I 'member sittin' a lot
back when I was 10 years old
I didn't have much choice,
always waitin' on a bench by the road,
sometimes for hours, mostly alone,
but the aides would check on me
now and then.

Chapter Ten
Artists, Writers, Entertainers, and More

Lewis Cross's 1934 painting of passenger pigeons

Born in 1863 in Genesee County, Michigan, **Lewis Cross** eight years later came to Spring Lake with his parents. He made his living as a farmer, fruit grower, hunter, fisherman, and taxidermist, but his true passion was art. Five hundred to six hundred of his paintings were sold at auction after his suicide at the age of 88. Many of the paintings lamented the slaughter of the passenger pigeons that once filled the skies of West Michigan. Restaurants touted pigeon as a delicacy and they were harvested by the barrelful to satisfy the appetites of diners throughout the Midwest. Professional hunters killed hundreds of thousands of passenger pigeons for the lucrative restaurant market, and milliners sought the bird's kaleidoscope of feathers. Cross, both naturalist and artist, underscored the importance of conservation in his oil paintings. To emphasize his point, Lewis painted the birds on canvases as large as eleven by eight feet. In the next photograph, Lewis is standing in front of the concrete-block home he built over a four year period and remains standing today. [Painting by Lewis Cross, photograph courtesy of Gwen Noren.]

Lewis Cross in front of his self-built home

Winsor McCay

Spring Lake native **Winsor McCay** became best known for his comic strips, especially "Little Nemo in Slumberland." The cartoon first appeared once a week in the *New York Herald* in 1905, ran for the next nine years, was syndicated throughout the U.S. and Europe, and then had a short revival between 1924 and 1926. McCay was considered one of the finest draftsman of comic art. His strip was the first to be honored with an exhibition at the Metropolitan Museum of Art in New York. He also was a circus poster painter, billboard painter, vaudeville performer, and editorial cartoonist. In 1913 he created one of his finest achievements, "Gertie the Dinosaur," the first animated cartoon to give life to its subject. He took his creation to the vaudeville stage and appeared with W. C. Fields and Houdini. [Sketch by Stephanie Grimm and courtesy of SLDL.]

THREE WHEELS AND HOME MADE

A three-wheeled automobile which has been driven 50 miles an hour and is used in daily service has been built by N. E. Brown of Grand Haven, Michigan. The total cost of construction was $100. Brown has driven the machine over 5,000 miles. He can turn a corner almost at right angles and can thread any thoroughfare with ease. With but one wheel in the rear, the vehicle insures easy riding and all ordinarily disagreeable bumps are eliminated.

Nat Brown in his three-wheel automobile

Nat Brown in his motor-driven sled

Photographer **Nat Brown** came to Grand Haven in the early 1900s. Prior to that he was a backwoods guide in Minnesota. Nat claimed to be the first photographer to get "bird's eyes views" of local scenes by attaching a camera to a kite, long before the advent of aerial photography. Many of his early photographs were made into postcards, which still are in circulation and sought by collectors. Nat created "Life Motion Photographs," by which a viewer can put an image into motion by moving his head "to and fro," as the instructions phrase it. He devised a propeller-powered sled, shown here, a propeller-driven motor boat, and a three-wheeled automobile, seen in the advertisement above, with Nat in the driver's seat. He also is the driver pictured on the sled. A hunter and trapper, Nat was in contact with Commander Robert Byrd to furnish a specialized toboggan for one of the explorer's Arctic trips. Nat also received a patent for a gyroplane in 1912. In 1938 he was accused and convicted of dynamiting his former home on Potawatomie Bayou. He said he had been cheated in a real estate transaction. Nat died in 1938 at the age of 72. [First photograph courtesy of WE, second photograph courtesy of Ron Kuiper.]

Henry Clubb

Henry Clubb, born in 1827 in England, immigrated to America in 1853. He moved to Kansas, where he established a Vegetarian Settlement Company [Vegetarian Kansas Emigration Company] in Neosho County. One evening, while on business in Ft. Scott, Kansas, Henry was threatened by a crowd opposed to his abolitionist views. Henry "looked them in the eye" and told them, "Well, gentleman, your numbers are sufficient to put any threat into execution, and I am among you alone and unprotected. If you require me to leave, I must, under the circumstances, do so, but it is rather late, being after sundown, and if tomorrow morning would suit you as well, it will be a good deal better, as I intend to leave then." He was allowed to leave on his own schedule. The next year he settled in Grand Haven, where he published and edited the *Ottawa Clarion*. The *Clarion* was issued until the fall of 1862, when Henry joined the United States Volunteer Service as Captain and Assistant Quartermaster. He was wounded at Corinth, Mississippi and was discharged in 1866. In 1867 he became Alderman for the Fourth Ward of Grand Haven's first City Council and a school commissioner. In 1873 and 1874 he served in the Michigan Senate, and in 1873 he was Secretary to the Michigan Constitutional Convention. In 1869 Henry began publication of the *Grand Haven Herald*. In 1876 he was called to be Pastor of the Bible Christian Church in Philadelphia. In Philadelphia Clubb, by then a noted vegetarian, became editor of a magazine titled *Food, Home, and Garden*. He died in Philadelphia in 1921. [Photograph courtesy of TCHM.]

In 1915 **David Cable** of Grand Haven published the poem "Rosy Mound," concerning the tall sand dune south of the city. In the photograph, Cable is seated in the front row wearing glasses, posing with other members of his family. His poem reads in part:

> One mile from Grand Haven town,
> Is a hill they call Rosy Mound;
> As a country resort,
> It is very much renowned;
> This Rosy Mound is quite steep,
> Some three hundred feet above the ground;

And when you get up there,
You can see for miles around . . .;
When you get to the top,
You'll think it very nice,
You can look out over the lake,
See the waves as they break.
Take in the scenery all around . . . ,
This mound was covered with flowers,
And you could sit there for hours,
But they took away more than their share,
Now there is hardly any more there.

[Photograph courtesy of TCHM.]

David Cable and family

After visiting the Grand Haven area for several years, poet **Edgar Lee Masters** in the summer of 1916 rented a cottage on Spring Lake. In his autobiography he noted that he wrote much of *Spoon River Anthology* while vacationing there. Edgar, who had a law practice in Chicago, in 1917 bought a twelve-acre farm on Spring Lake. The farm included a fruit orchard and frontage on the lake. He stayed at nearby Arbutus Banks, a summer hotel, while the farm was updated. While sitting on the shore of Spring Lake, Edgar wrote several poems about the Grand River, Grand Haven, and the lumbering industry. One of his poems, "Grand River Marshes," contained this verse:

> But all is quiet on the river now
> As when the snow lay windless in the wood,
> And the last Indian stood
> And looked to find the broken bough
> That told the path under the snow.
> All is as silent as the spiral lights
> Of purple and of gold that from the marshes rise,
> Like the wings of swarming dragon flies,
> Far up toward Eastmanville, where the enclosing skies
> Quiver with heat; as silent as the flights
> Of the crow like smoke from shops against the glare
> Of dunes and purple air,
> There where Grand Haven against the sand hill lies.

In 1970 the United State Post Office issued a stamp in his memory. [Image courtesy of WE.]

**Edgar Lee Masters
postage stamp**

Stewart Edward White

After spending his early years in Grand Haven, **Stewart Edward White**, a descendant of Rev. William and Amanda Ferry, moved with his parents to Grand Rapids in the late 1870s. He earned bachelor and master degrees from the University of Michigan, and then spent eight or ten years in lumber camps and on the rivers where he gained the background for his novels. Stewart enlisted in the Army at the start of WWI and was given the rank of Major of U.S. Field Artillery. He became a well-known author of such works as *Blazed Trails*, *The Riverman*, *Daniel Boone*, and *Wilderness Scout*. Twelve of his novels and short stories were made into movies, mostly during the era of the silent films. A 1941 film, *Wild Geese Calling*, starring Henry Fonda, was based on one of his novels. As a result of White's study of bird life, several hundred stuffed birds were preserved in the Kent Scientific Museum [now Grand Rapids Public Museum]. [Photograph courtesy of WE.]

Leonard "Red" Bird

Born in California in 1936, **Leonard "Red" Bird** was one of 900 marines ordered to witness the detonation of a nuclear weapon at Yucca Flats in 1952. Exposure to extreme levels of radiation caused the cancer that took his life in 2010. Red taught English at Fort Lewis College in Colorado, where he was on the faculty for 31 years. He authored three books: *River of Lost Souls*, *The Scorned Ally*, and *Folding Paper Cranes, an Atomic Memoir*. After retirement, he and his wife, Jane, moved to Grand Haven. [Photograph courtesy of Jane Leonard.]

Twins **Herbert and Howard Lyman** of Grand Haven and Spring Lake formed a comedy team in the late 1890s and performed vaudeville acts for 15 years. Born in Grand Haven, they were the sons of Charles and Mary Lyman and the grandsons of Lucius Lyman. The twins first performed professionally in 1897 touring with the Holden Comedy Company. They headlined their debut musical comedy as writers and performers in 1898 in the play *Money to Burn*. The brothers wrote and performed six more original musical comedies nationwide before retiring from theater in early 1912. Eventually they both moved to Orlando, Florida and purchased orange groves. [Photograph courtesy of Kevin Collier.]

Herbert and Howard Lyman

Jackie Band

In 1913 **Andy Thomson** organized the Jackie Band. Consisting of 24 boys the Band made its first appearance in a Memorial Day parade that year, playing "Three Cheers for the Red, White, and Blue." The group wore white uniforms, trimmed in purple. Later, their outfits were changed to blue and white, similar to those used by the Navy, and a Navy style cap was added. The new outfits were called "Jackies," and that gave the group its name. The Band appeared at Liberty Loan Drives during WWI, played at the departure and homecoming of soldiers, performed in neighboring towns, and held concerts in Grand Haven's Central Park. Eventually the band grew to 64 members, all boys. The band dissolved in 1924, when the Grand Haven High School Band was formed. Thomson is standing in the upper right with baton in hand. [Photograph courtesy of TCHM.]

Coppins and Adelaide Carew

In 1930 **Coppins Carew** was a waiter at the Ferry Hotel in downtown Grand Haven at the same time his parents owned and operated the Grand Haven Chicken Inn a block over on Franklin Street. Coppins and his brother Ben formed a dance team for a brief time, but Ben, who played the drums, preferred to perform with a local orchestra. Adelaide Fox was born in Minnesota about 1912 and married Coppins when she was 16. Coppins took dancing lessons from Bojangles [Bill Robinson, 1878-1949], and then, in turn, taught Adelaide. The two danced on Mississippi showboats and in night clubs in Chicago and other Midwest cities. [Photograph courtesy of Carew family.]

Olaf Gylleck

Olaf Gylleck, a professional magician, appeared in vaudeville acts in his early years. He learned the printing trade to supplement his income and was employed by Challenge Machinery in Grand Haven. Olaf traveled to Printing House Craftsman Clubs around the country, giving a 20-minute technical talk about Challenge products followed by a 40-minute magic show. He continued to perform for clubs in West Michigan after retirement from Challenge. A brochure announced, "Gylleck's presentation is a strictly refined and educational amusement, by a personable, polished performer. You will like it!" [Photograph courtesy of Bob Verduin.]

"Congratulations, Chuck. It is unfortunate that your record is not better. You need to improve in the years to come." Those words, emblazoned in Charles Westover's 1953 yearbook, were written by a teacher in reference to Chuck's reputation for underachievement and misbehavior. The young hipster had purchased a used guitar for $5. Like an imaginary friend, the guitar would be ever-present to the annoyance of school staff who interpreted it as rebellious, attention-seeking nonsense. In 1953 there was far more concern for Chuck's future than appreciation for his music, but rural Coopersville's identity as a community would one day focus on this most unlikely native son.

Chuck's talents expanded from guitarist to singer and lyricist. His agent suggested a name change, and a rock star was born. Newly hailed "**Del Shannon**" released "Runaway" in February, 1961. By April it was #1 on *Billboard*. "Hats Off to Larry," "Little Town Flirt," "Handy Man," "Do You Want to Dance," and many more recordings soon followed. Shannon became a household name in the United States, but was even more popular in Europe. He shared the bill with the up and coming *Beatles* at London's Royal Albert Hall in 1963. Legal and liquor problems eventually were his undoing. In 1990 56-year old Del discharged a .22 caliber round into his skull. Today the small town of Coopersville hosts an annual festival to celebrate Del's music and classic cars of his era. The recording star was inducted into the Rock and Roll Hall of Fame in 1999. That's quite a *record*.
[Photograph courtesy of MV.]

Del Shannon gold record

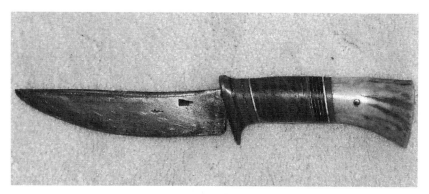

A William Scagel knife

William Scagel began his career as a bridge builder and wrought iron craftsman. After two failed marriages, he headed for the isolation of northern lumber camps, where in 1910 he began making knives. Later Bill honed his skills in a small shop in Muskegon and eventually relocated to Fruitport. By 1920 Scagel was emerging as an uncommon bladesmith among knife aficionada. He sold camp and sport knives, fighting knives, pocket knives, and related hardware to Abercrombie and Fitch in New York and other upscale dealers. His sharpware was used on Smithsonian expeditions. He is regarded as "The Father of 20th Century Cutlery." As one who profoundly influenced the cutlery trade for over a century, Bill was inducted into the Blade Cutlery Hall of Fame. A number of factors make Scagel knives the standard by which all others are measured. First, after having heated words with the power company, Bill pulled the plug at his "Dogwood Nub" home and shop in Fruitport. His knives were then made with power he squeezed out of an old windmill, submarine batteries, and a gas engine connected to a system of pulleys and belts.

William Scagel's workshop

Bill selected only the strongest steel for his knives. The artistry in his stag horn and leather grips was unmatched; the grip itself was contoured to the human hand before anyone had heard the word *ergonomic*. There were few straight edges in Scagel knife design, only subtle curves melting into the hand. Scagel knives have exceeded $20,000 in value. A legend in the cutlery trade and a social recluse, Scagel died a poor man in 1963 at age ninety. [Photographs courtesy of MV.]

Carlotta Parthenia Walkley Bailey was the daughter of Wyllys S. Walkley, who became a Grand Haven physician. After her mother died when she was two years old, Carlotta was raised by foster parents on a farm near Grand Rapids while her father attended medical school. She graduated from Hillsdale Academy and, in 1892, from Hillsdale College as valedictorian. After marriage to A. E. Ewing she appeared throughout Michigan as an elocutionist and reader of dramatic and humorous literature. She earned a master degree from the University of Michigan in 1916 and subsequently was employed by Child and Family Services to visit the homes of foster children.

Carlotta Parthenia Walkley Bailey Ewing

In 1910 Carlotta and her husband bought 30 acres on Lake Michigan, not far from Rosy Mound, and built a cottage. Ten years later they sold that property and purchased 199 acres about two miles farther south, an area still called the "Wilderness." The natural wooded beauty of the dunes and the expansive beach made the Wilderness attractive to others, and it became a second home to many Grand Rapids residents. The land had been well lumbered in the previous century, and by 1922 the second growth of beech, oak, and pine trees had reached a respectable size. Ewing controlled the sale of the lots in the Wilderness, vetting prospective buyers to make sure they adhered to the same environmental standards she did: all cottage were to be built behind the tree line in order to protect the dunes and to maintain the natural look of the land. She died in 1971, a few months after her 100th birthday. [Photograph courtesy of WE.]

Born in 1912, **Chuck Bugielski** moved to Grand Haven with his parents in the mid-1920s. After graduating from Grand Haven High School in 1930, he was hired by McLellan Dime Store in Grand Haven as stockman. On August 18, 1933, he played a role in thwarting a robbery at Peoples Bank and Trust. In 1938 Chuck left his job at McLellan's and opened the M & M Variety Store, located first at 706 Washington and by 1944 at 711 Washington. For the 100th birthday of Grand Haven in 1934 the 22-year old was asked to help expand the annual Coast Guard picnic. Although meant to be a one-time event, the Coast Guard Festival evolved into today's annual community observance. Bugielski managed the festivities with Glenn Eaton and Claude Ver Duin from 1947 to 1981. The back office of his store served as the Coast Guard Festival's office from 1938 to 1981. Chuck volunteered for the March of Dimes for 20 years, led the Community Chest Fund, was President of the Grand Haven Chamber of Commerce and Rotary from 1950-51, and belonged to the Eagles. [Photograph courtesy of Tri-Cities Chamber of Commerce.]

Chuck Bugielski

Jessie Olsen and her court

Jessie Olsen of Grand Haven in 1939 was selected the first-ever U.S. Coast Guard Queen. Appropriate to her heritage, she joined the SPARS during WWII. Jessie's sister, Betty, was part of the Queen's Court during Grand Haven's Centennial Celebration in August, 1934. Jessie and her husband, John H. Cole, moved to Houghton Lake. Jessie lived from 1923 to 1995. [Photograph courtesy of TCHM.]

Joseph "Pop" Davis and friends

The Barn, shown in this picture postcard, offered dancing, roller skating, pinball machines, duck pin bowling, ping pong, and other forms of recreation until it burned down in the spring of 1946. Among the big bands that played to big crowds at the Barn were Gene Krupa, Jack Teagarden, Earl Hines, Ted Weems, and Fats Waller. The large frame structure had once served as a warehouse. In the early 1920s it was moved in three sections by barge down the Grand River to approximately 215 South Harbor Drive. Pop Davis, pictured in the inset on the left, bought the Barn from Nat Robbins in 1934. The young man on the right Joe Davis, Jr., helped manage the recreational center. [Photograph courtesy of WE.]

Bruce Matthews

Born in 1904, **Bruce Matthews** designed and renovated more than 100 golf courses. He earned national and state recognition for developing challenging but playable courses. He once said, "The easiest thing to do is build a tough hole. To build a course people enjoy is another story." Matthews purchased 235 acres in Grand Haven Township, and in 1964 he opened the 18-hole Grand Haven Golf Club. He also platted and sold building sites along Timberdunes Drive, which divides the golf course. His son, Wally, took over the management two years later and continued in that capacity until the family sold the course in 1998. Among his other activities, Matthews established the Turfgrass Foundation at Michigan State University and he helped launch a golf shop management curriculum at Ferris State University. [Photograph courtesy of Bruce Matthews III.]

Neal Ball

After playing the minor leagues, **Neal Ball** spent seven seasons with the New York Highlanders, forerunner of the Yankees, the Cleveland Indians, and the Boston Red Sox. A right-handed hitter, Neal was best remembered for completing the first unassisted triple play in the American League. That occurred on July 19, 1909, when he was playing shortstop for the Indians. He snagged a line drive, doubled one Red Sox player off second base, and then tagged the runner coming in from first. Neal hit an inside-the-park homerun in the same game. He maintained a .251 batting average for the 496 games of his major league career. He returned to the minor leagues in 1914, and he was manager from time to time until his full retirement from the game in 1922. Neal, who stood five feet seven inches and weighed 145 pounds, was born in Grand Haven in 1881 and died in Bridgeport, Connecticut in 1957. [Image courtesy of Wikipedia.]

Will Larson's log cabin

In 1916 **Will Larson**, son of resort entrepreneur Charles Larson, pitched the idea of hosting West Michigan's first marathon. To secure the event for Grand Haven and to lure competitors into a stay at the family's Log Cabin Club, Larson convinced the Chamber of Commerce to furnish "suitable prizes" for the nationally ranked athletes they would attract. A twenty mile course was plotted by "good roads" advocate William Connelly. Starting at Muskegon's Occidental Hotel, the route would take runners through Fruitport, Spring Lake, and Ferrysburg on to Grand Haven where the finish line lay at the foot of Washington Street.

Runners gathered in anticipation of the blast from Muskegon Mayor Ellison's gun. The large crowd delivered a rousing send-off. A hotfooted lad named Mellar took the early lead. On the brink of collapse near Third and Fulton in Grand Haven, Mellar's trainer prodded him on as "Costopaulis the Greek" threatened to pass him. In the end neither of the exhausted men could keep pace. Two hours, twelve minutes, and eight seconds into the race, Sidney Hatch, one of the greatest runners in the United States, thrust himself across the finish line.

Competitors happily returned to Larson's Log Cabin Club, pictured here, on Potawatomie Bayou for rest, recuperation, and recreation. Amenities included a bathing beach, boat and angling gear rentals, a fine dining facility, rooms and cabins, not to mention the modern telephone. Racers praised their hosts and pledged to return in 1917 for what promised to be an annual Midwest classic. It would not happen, for a greater contest was brewing in Germany on the eve of WWI. [Postcard image courtesy of WE.]

George and Effie Miller's gravestone

George and Effie Miller literally took their beloved "Log Cabin" to the grave. Etched in their headstone at Lake Forest Cemetery in Grand Haven is an image of their historic Potawatomie Bayou home. The land at 15197 Lake Avenue was purchased by Christine Larson of Chicago for $500 in 1908. Her husband Charles, a competent carpenter, millwright, and contractor, built the modest summer cabin fastened simply by wooden pegs and chinking. The interior logs were lacquered, giving them a dark, shiny patina that added to the cabin's cozy appeal. The Larsons entertained throngs of friends and family who delighted in the lakeside setting and recreational resources. When Charles died the next year, the place was sold to the Carl Wahlbergs, and was billed thereafter as the "Log Cabin Hotel on Potawatomie Lake." Its popularity faded and the property drifted among owners.

In 1955 George and Effie Miller purchased the historic site for $12,000. Its hotel roots were perfect for accommodating the growing Miller family, who fully appreciated the rustic ambiance of the old club. Their stewardship spanned across four decades. Advancing in age and now empty nesters, it became increasingly difficult for the Millers to maintain the log home and its expansive grounds. They sold the property in the late 1990s for $200,000 to a contractor who razed the cabin. George died in 2005. Effie followed in 2009. The land remains vacant, but their much-loved Log Cabin home will be remembered by all who visit George's and Effie's gravesite. [Photograph courtesy of Kathy Miller Van Houwelingen.]

Allen and Julia Cordes

In the mid-1920s **Allen and Julia Cordes** purchased a 40-acre farm on North Cedar Drive in Robinson Township, where they constructed a barn in 1928. Three years later they converted the barn to a restaurant and dance hall named Jac Jungle. The initials of his wife's name, Julia A. Cordes, supplied the word "Jac." A grandson later said of Julia, "She was boss, but you couldn't help loving her. She was only about five feet tall, but the best bouncer Jac Jungle had." In addition to food and dancing, the popular night spot featured such special events as a balloon ascension, parachutists, and vaudeville acts. Local band leaders, Bob Warnaar and Doug Baker, both played there. Warnaar said he insisted on chicken wire to protect his band from flying objects. The Cordeses sold the property in 1941. [Photograph courtesy of Barb Nelson.]

One of the acts at Jac Jungle

Chapter Eleven
People with Unique Stories

George Zysk building a tree house

"If you were a kid again, what would be your idea of the best of all possible playhouses?" A newspaper reporter in 1960 posed this question to his readers, as part of an interview with **George Zysk** of Grand Haven. A news photo caught George putting the finishing touches on the tree house pictured here. He built it for his son at the family home on Jackson Street. Zysk also was well known as the "sign man," a reference to the political statements and Bible verses he painted on the exterior of his house for about 20 years. [Photograph courtesy of WE.]

Fred Graves

Fred Graves, a former slave, in 1898 spoke to the Woman's Club in Grand Haven. He recounted an occasion when 500 slaves were advertised for sale. Chained to one another, they were taken to a slave market where Fred and his mother were sold for $1,200. He escaped from his Virginia owner, but was found and returned. Two years later he escaped again by hiding in a haystack for five days. Fred said that prior to his successful escape he was a servant on the Confederate side at the First Battle of Bull Run, but joined the Union side in time for the Second Battle of Bull Run after his haystack experience. He also attended General Burnside and acted as a bodyguard for General Phillip Sheridan. After the war, Fred and his wife, Isabella, relocated to Grand Haven. They worked at Sheldon's Mineral Springs Resort, located where Fifth Third Bank now does business. Fred lived from 1835 to 1921 and was buried at Lake Forest Cemetery. [Photograph courtesy of TCHM.]

Wilford Dake and fellow prospectors

In 1890 the twelve men pictured here left West Michigan to search for gold in the Copper River Country of Alaska. Joining them was seventeen-year old **Wilford Dake** of Grand Haven, second from the right in the front row. Wilford's mother said her son was too young to be part of the expedition, but the men declared they would look after him. Two other Grand Haven residents, Peter and Fred vanden Berg, also also joined the group. Both were a few years older than Wilford. After Wilford's return to Grand Haven, apparently empty-handed, he opened a shop at 213 Second Street in Grand Haven where he sold, repaired, and raced bicycles. Wilford died in 1913, only 40 years old. His father, William F. Dake, one of the founders of Dake Engine Company of Grand Haven, died at the age of 42.
[Photograph courtesy of David Vandermolen.]

Marjorie Correll

In this 1936 news photograph, **Marjorie Correll** is at Lake Forest Cemetery, admiring the ornate and unusual tombstone of John Quayle, a sailor, who died in Chicago of pneumonia in 1882. He was buried under the large concrete monument adorned with nautical symbols and the word "Mizpah," meaning "watchtower" in Hebrew. The monument, with its distinctive tree stump and nautical theme, was manufactured by the F. O. Gross Company of Chicago for deceased members of Modern Woodmen of America. John's parents were residents of Grand Haven, and Marjorie's connection with the family may be through the Woodmen organization.
[Photograph courtesy of WE.]

John Vyn at Vyn Company headquarters

John Vyn worked in the family trucking business, Derk Vyn & Son, located at 225 Fulton Avenue. In 1921 while making deliveries in Spring Lake, it looked as if a train would hit the slow-moving Vyn truck in which John was a passenger. Vyn jumped out of the cab to save himself. The driver accelerated and was able to get across the tracks, but John became entangled and was hit by the train. He left a wife and two children. He is the tallest of the four men standing in the center of the photograph. [Photograph courtesy of TCHM.]

Benjamin Campbell, Jr., and classmates

Benjamin Campbell, Jr., who was born on April 28, 1867, died of peritonitis in Spring Lake on February 8, 1883. One of the few early African Americans in Spring Lake Village, Benjamin was the son of a shoe cobbler, who ran a successful business in the Village. Benjamin, shown with his classmates, graduated from the eighth grade in 1881. [Image courtesy of the Kitchel family.]

Matilda Dushane's grave site

When **Matilda Dushane** died of cholera in 1872, only eleven days old, she was buried on the family farm in Grand Haven Township. In 1930 Lakeshore Drive was extended south, taking the new route over Matilda's gravesite. Lorraine Orsinger, a Dushane descendant, protested its planned removal and prevailed. The fenced-in grave is on the east side of the road, south of Hiawatha Street. [Photograph courtesy of WE.]

In 1907, **Dick Gringhuis, Sr.** married Margje Van Doorne in Grand Haven. Two months before the birth of their son, the 29-year old father died of peritonitis, the result of an accident at the William Heap factory, where he was employed. Heap & Son produced plumbing supplies. Shown here is the floral arrangement sent by Dick's classmates for the funeral. His portrait, dwarfed by the arrangement, is in the center. [Photograph courtesy of Wanda Anderson.]

Dick Gringhuis, Sr. floral arrangement

Dick Gringhuis, Jr.

Dick Gringhuis, Jr., was born in Grand Haven on December 24, 1907, three months after his father's death. Young Dick was at his aunt's house on the night of his fourth birthday, Christmas Eve, 1911. The family was quarantined because his cousin Peter had scarlet fever. The presents under the tree in the second photograph above were all for young Dick. [Photograph courtesy of Wanda Anderson.]

Robert White

Robert White of Grand Haven worked for one of the local railroads as Section Foreman. As a hobby and for extra income, he produced postcards. On the back of his advertising postcards shown here Bob told prospective customers, "It cost 25 cents for a negative for Personal Cards like this and 5 cents each for any number of cards from it." Bob was only 52 years old when he died in 1976. [Photograph courtesy of WE.]

In 1891 Dr. Henry Dubee married **Marian Vander Veen**, shown here inside her home at 508 Washington Street. The daughter of Dr. Arend Vander Veen, Marian continued to reside in the family home until her death in 1973 at the age of 103. The home was not equipped with electricity until after her death. As a young girl, Marian recalled that when her father was out on sick calls, her mother mounted the stairway shown in the photograph and climbed to the top of the tower in their home to signal him with a lantern, letting him know there was an emergency call. [Photograph courtesy of TCHM.]

Marian Vander Veen Dubee

Tom Mahon operated a pile driver on the Grand River before going to Chicago to set pilings at the 1893 Columbian Exposition for the world's first Ferris Wheel. After returning to Grand Haven, Mahon became a diver. In the photograph he is rising from the depths of Government Basin in 1917. He worked for the Corps of Engineers and received his pilot and engineering license in 1908. At age 82 he helped lay cable for the City of Holland. [Photograph courtesy of WE.]

Tom Mahon

On August 18, 1933 at 2:55 in the afternoon Edward Bentz, Jimmy "Baby Face" Nelson, Chuck Fisher, and Tommy Carrol walked into Peoples Bank and Trust in downtown Grand Haven. They must have looked suspicious, because shortly after they walked in bank teller Art Welling pressed the foot alarm that sounded in the furniture store next door. Hearing the alarm Edward Kinkema and Chuck Bugielski responded by grabbing guns and going to the street to meet the robbers as they came out of the bank. Kinkema met the getaway car driver, pointed his shotgun and ordered the man known only as Freddie to get out of the city. In the meantime the robbers were apprehensive of the people gathering in the street, curious why the bank was closing early. Taking bank employees with them the robbers went out the back door to be met with gunfire from Kinkema and Bugielski. The confusion that resulted gave **Fredrick C. "Ted" Bolt** an opportunity to try to wrestle the gun away from the outside man, Earl Doyle. Doyle was shot twice when Kinkema charged in to help Bolt confiscate his gun. The rest of the robbers fled down Third Street and commandeered a Chevrolet driven by a woman and carrying another woman and three children as passengers. The robbers then made their getaway in the stolen car. Inside the bank, four citizens were injured by gunfire. The only other man captured in the robbery was Theodore Bentz, who denied that he had participated in the robbery, but was convicted nevertheless.

Born in Grand Haven in 1897, Ted graduated from the University of Michigan School of Business Administration and was a WWI veteran. He and others shared a $1,000 reward for stopping the robbery while it was in progress, despite the flying bullets. Ted went on to become President of the Bank in 1944. [Photograph courtesy of TCHM.]

Frederick C. Bolt

In 1846 the Reverend **Thomas Carlton** family left New York for Grand Haven. Arriving in Grand Rapids, Mrs. Carlton succumbed to smallpox. The Reverend then engaged a driver, oxen, and sleigh to transport his infected family. The journey through the woods was complicated by deep snow and freezing temperatures, making River Road [Leonard Road] impassable, as one might imagine in the scene pictured here. News of disease preceded the group, and upon arrival in Eastmanville, they were driven out by terrified townsmen. The wayfarers sought shelter at Realy's and Miller's Midway House Inn a short distance away. Unfortunately, the structure had been disassembled and was being moved from the south to the north side of River Road. Disappointment turned disaster when one of their exhausted oxen dropped dead. The despondent travelers themselves collapsed near William Nickerson's cabin, located on the Realy/Miller property. "Old Bill Nick" took them in and threatened to shoot any who dared interfere with the aid and comfort he alone offered. Despite Nickerson's heroic efforts, both Carlton and his nine-month-old son died. Reverend and Mrs. Carlton's daughters, aged three and six, recovered under Bill's care. Eventually they were reunited with extended family members in New York. This site, where long ago trapper William Nickerson offered shelter for thousands to follow in its transformations from humble cabin to roadhouse to poor house to infirmary to Community Haven and to county park where people find respite today. [Painting by Joseph Farquharson.]

Painting by Joseph Farquharson

Index

Aiken, Eddie, 122
Aiken, George, 30, 122
Ainsworth, Dewitt, 103
Akeley, Healey, 35
Allen, John, 21
Baker, Derk, 45
Baker, Doug, 146
Ball, Angie, 26
Ball, Gerrit, 61
Ball, John, 26
Ball, Jurrien, 61
Ball, Neal, 143
Bareham, Eunice Keskey, 97
Bareham, Robert, 97
Barrett, Ruby, 41
Barrett, William, 41
Bement, Harley, 98
Bethke, Robert, 106
Beukema, Henry, 78
Bilz, Aloys, 52
Bird, Leonard "Red", 131
Blakeslee, Chauncey, 93
Blount, Harvey, 118
Boer, Henry, 63
Bolt, Frederick "Ted", 157
Boon, Marge, 96
Boon, Martin, 45
Bottje, Clifford, 53
Bottje, Edward, 53
Bottje, Gerrit, 53
Bottje, Jeanette, 70
Bottje, Mary, 70
Bourassa, Charlotte, 11
Bowen, Carl, 93
Boyden, Charles, 60
Braak, Jacob, 56
Braak, Jennie Reenders, 56
Briggs, Eliza Wood, 98
Brinkert, Les, 95
Brown, Cyril, 81
Brown, Nat, 126
Bugielski, Chuck, 48, 139, 157
Cable, David, 127
Campbell, Benjamin, Jr., 151
Carew, Adelaide Fox, 134

Carew, Ben, 134
Carew, Coppins, 134
Carlton, Mrs., 158
Carlton, Thomas, 158
Cawne, Louis (Louise).
Cawne, Pierre, 12
Christman, George, 44
Clubb, Henry, 127
Conklin, Charles, 104
Connelly, William, 93, 144
Constant, Lisette (Louise), 12
Cooper, John, 120
Cordes, Allen, 146
Cordes, Julia, 146
Correll, Marjorie, 150
Cutler, Dwight, 27, 90
Dake, Wilford, 62, 149
Daley, Pat, 108
Danhof, Marie, 89
Danhof, Peter, 89
Davis, Joseph "Pop", 141
Davis, Joseph, Jr., 141
Deetjen, Larry, 96
DeLand, Colonel, 23
Deremo, Dorothy, 31, 32
Deremo, Harry, 31, 32
Dickinson, Otis Bowman, 69
Dornbos, Gerrit, 46
Dornbos, Henry J., 46
Dubee, Henry, 155
Duncan, Robert, 88
Dunham, Major, 89
Dushane, Mathilda, 152
Duvernay, Pierre, 16
Duvernay, William B. "Chid", 23
Eastman, Timothy, 21
Eaton, Glenn, 48, 139
Eaton, Monroe, 119
Ekkens, Gerrit, 58
Erickson, Martin, 58
Ericson, E. Vincent, 105
Everett, Franklin, 25
Ewing, A. E., 138
Ewing, Carlotta Walkley Bailey, 138
Ferry, Amanda White, 92

Ferry, William, 14, 16, 17, 21, 92, 117, 118
Fisher, Elmer, 107
Flahive, Scott, 112
Ford, Gerald, 106
Fortino, Louis, 57
Gardner, Eugene, 99
Gidley, Townsend, 29, 30
Graves, Fred, 148
Graves, Isabella, 148
Gringhuis, Dick, Jr., 153
Gringhuis, Dick, Sr., 153
Gylleck, Olaf, 135
Hall, Winfield Sscott, 83
Hancock, George, 33
Harbeck, Herman, 37
Harbin, Keith, 112
Harper, William, 70
Hatton, Elizabeth, 38
Hatton, William, 38
Hidden, Helen, 107
Hofma, Edward, 82
Hopkins, Claude, 40
Huntington, Martha, 88
Hunton, David Fletcher, 121
Johnson, Paul, 42, 105
Jones, Benjamin, 15, 117
Jubb, Edward, 101
Jubb, Moline, 101
Kedgnal, John Henry [John Henry Duvernay], 23
Kieft, William, 54
Kinkema, Edward, 157
Kirk, Harry, 94
Kitchel, John, 84
Kitchel, Mary Spurgeon, 84
Klempel, Emil, 111
Klempel, Richard, 111
Kooiman, Henry, 59
Koster, Agnes, 73
La Framboise, Joseph, 12
La Framboise, Magdalene, 17
Langlade, Charles, 11
Larson, Christine, 145
Larson, Will, 144
Lasley, William, 13

Leonard, Jane, 131
Lillie, Hugh, 87
Lillie, Leo, 87
Littooij, Maria, 114
Loutit, William, 105
Lyman, Charles, 132
Lyman, Herbert, 132
Lyman, Howard, 132
Lyman, Lucius, 132
Lyman, Mary, 132
Mahon, Tom, 156
Mansfield, Mary K. Rice, 69
Marcotte, Jean Baptiste, 12
Marcotte, Timothee, 12
Martin, Henry, 90
Masters, Edgar Lee, 129
Matthews, Bruce, 142
McCay, Winsor, 125
McNett, Eleanor Griffin, 91
Meyer, Frank, 76
Miller, Daniel, 108
Miller, David, 108
Miller, Effie, 145
Miller, Elizabeth Realy, 108, 113
Miller, George, 145
Miller, Harry, 19
Miller, Harry (Henry), 113
Miller, Henry "Harry", 108
Miller, Henry, Jr., 113
Miller, Mary Daniels, 114
Morgan, Henry, 21
Morse, Elsie, 51
Morse, Thomas, 51
Motspie, Chief, 113
Mulder, Alice, 62
Mulder, Elizabeth, 62
Mulder, Klaas, 34, 51
Mulder, Lambertus, 62
Nevins, Fleda, 74
Nickerson, William, 158
Nyland, Esther Dean, 75
Oakes, James, 63
Olsen, Jessie, 140
O'Malley, Raymond, 109
Ossinger, Lorraine, 152
Pagelsen, Charles, 91

Parker, Anna, 98
Parrisien, Jean Baptiste, 20
Pennoyer, Harriet, 22
Pennoyer, Henry, 22, 24
Pennoyer, Lettie Teeple Rellingston, 22, 24
Pruim, Elizabeth, 82
Pytlinske, Felix, 49
Quayle, John, 150
Quinterri, Chiara, 57
Realy, Daniel, 19, 113
Regester, Bruce, 123
Reichardt, John, 60
Rellingston, Sarah Jane, 24
Rellingston, William, 24
Rice, James, 69
Rice, Margaret, 69
Rice, Mattie, 69
Robbins, Nat, 93
Robbins, Nathaniel, 65
Robinson, Ira, 102
Robinson, Rix, 12, 14, 17, 21, 102
Rogers, George, 86
Rutty, Monroe, 119
Rycenga, Chuck, Jr., 55
Rycenga, Chuck, Sr., 55
Rycenga, Louis, 55
Savidge, Hunter, 27, 44, 52, 90
Scagel, William, 137
Schmedtgen, Herman, 50
Schmidt, Dorothea, 34
Schmidt, William, 34
Scholten, Harvey, 105
Schultz, Elfrieda, 49
Scott, James, 63
Shabart, Elmer, 85
Shannon, Del, 136
Sickman, Joe, 110
Skinner, Ida, 79
Smallman, Agnes, 66

Smallman, Joshua, 66
Smith, Edmon, 15
Smith, Lawrence, 120
Soule, Julia, 71
Spadafore, Charlie, 57
Stansberry, Warren, 39
Stark, Margaret, 76
Steel, Joe, 119
Story, Hampton, 36
Stuart, Robert, 14, 17, 29
Swart, George, 59
Thomson, Andy, 133
Uhl, John, 105
Van Doorne, Margje, 153
Van Kampen, Robert, 43
Van Schelven, John, 63
Van Zantwick, Govert, 64
Vander Sticht, Hendrika, 115
Vander Veen, Arend, 155
Vander Veen, Marian, 155
Vanderveen, Arend, 80
Vanderveen, Jacob, 61
Ver Duin, Claude, 48, 139
Ver Duin, John, 47
Ver Duin, Sena, 47
Verberkmoes, Cornelis, 67
Von Oettingen, Elizabeth "Liese", 77
Vyn, John, 151
Wahlberg, Carl, 145
Walkley, Wyllys, 79, 138
Warnaar, Bob, 146
Welling, Art, 157
Westover, Charles
  see Shannon, Del, 136
White, Mary, 68
White, Mary A., 25
White, Nathan, 18
White, Robert, 154
White, Stewart Edward, 130